WHO KNOWS?

Orangebooks Publication

1st Floor, Rajhans Arcade, Mall Road, Kohka, Bhilai, Chhattisgarh 490020

Website: **www.orangebooks.in**

© Copyright, 2025, Author

All rights reserved. No part of this book may be reproduced, stored in a retrieval system, or transmitted, in any form by any means, electronic, mechanical, magnetic, optical, chemical, manual, photocopying, recording or otherwise, without the prior written consent of its writer.

First Edition, 2025

ISBN: 978-93-6554-212-7

WHO KNOWS?

Lyncia Creado

OrangeBooks Publication
www.orangebooks.in

DEDICATIONS

This book is for you.

To the curious minds of tomorrow —

To the mothers who gave their all, to the fathers who tried their best, to the children who grew up too fast, and to the generations yet to come — may you laugh, learn, and find a little piece of yourself in these pages.

To God, who holds the past, present, and future in His hands.

And to the future itself — please be kind, and don't make me regret everything I wrote here.

ACKNOWLEDGEMENTS

This book wouldn't be possible without my incredible (and highly entertaining) family.

To my husband Astor, for putting up with my writing marathons and never asking, *"Are you done yet?"*

To my children, Shane, Thea, and Vanya — thank you for being the endless source of stories, laughter, inspiration, and prime book material! You should probably start negotiating royalties.

To my siblings Renuka & Ashwin, for the memories, mischief, and occasional blackmail-worthy moments.

To my late parents Nymphia & Hyginus, for their love, wisdom, and for passing down the storytelling gene.

To God, the ultimate author of our life stories, for His grace, wisdom, and the gift of words. Without Him, none of this would be possible.

I sincerely thank my daughter Thea for her meticulous proofreading of this book.

A special thank you to my talented daughter, Vanya, for designing the book cover. Your creativity and vision have brought *Who Knows* to life in a way that words alone never could.

TABLE OF CONTENTS

Introduction	1
Beyond Programming	3
A Mother Gives	6
Then – Now: Who Knows?	12
Rebooting	17
People, Tech & Staying True To Yourself	
• Plugging Into People	28
• Virtual Instantly	31
• The Metaverse	32
From Legends To Loops	34
Filters Vs. Reality	43
Where Logic Logs Out	49
What's In A Label	52
When Degrees Meet Deals	58
Mind Your Manners… Or Else!	63
Heaven's Hotline	68
Chic Or Shock	74
Why Get Married	78
Been There Done That	85
Slang Wars	90
Who Knows What Parents Say	95
Swipe Right At Your Own Risk	99
Dating & Dealing With 'The One'	109
Life Didn't Come Easy	121
A Night In The Mara	124
Lived & Let Live	129
Anchors Aweigh	134
Ctrl+Alt+Socialize	150
The Loyalty Test For Family Weddings	156

Shopping Cart Shenanigans	162
Internet Drama	
• The Great Password Crisis	166
• Household WiFi Wars	169
• GPS Betrayals	173
WhatsApp Family Groups	177
Mirror Mirror On The Wall	183
Oops! My Bad..	189
Wasn't It Just Yesterday	193

INTRODUCTION - A Letter To Tomorrow

Who Knows? As I sit down to write this book, I imagine you years from today, maybe curled up in a gravity-defying chair, scrolling through a holographic version on your smart lenses, or letting your AI assistant read it to you while you multitask between ten different things.
But these aren't just any stories. These are pieces of my family's history, lessons learned through love, struggle, and the occasional questionable decisions (like trusting GPS in the middle of nowhere or assuming one could survive prison stay unharmed (long story, we'll get there). It's also my way of passing on a little wisdom, wrapped in humour, because, if I just handed out life lessons without entertainment, you'd probably zone out.

Life will throw all sorts of things your way — some amazing, some challenging, and some so ridiculous that you'll wonder if you're trapped in a bad simulation. You'll deal with trends that make no sense (one day, neon eyebrows are cool; the next, they're banned), new vocabulary and moments where you're absolutely convinced you know everything. My children were the same.

This book is a time capsule of sorts — a collection of stories about my children's childhood antics, the games they played, and the values they learned (sometimes the easy way, but mostly the hard way). It's also a reminder that while technology will keep changing, some things will always matter — kindness, integrity, etiquette, prayer, family, and knowing when to mute an annoying group chat.

So, read with an open heart. Laugh at the funny bits (even at my expense), reflect on the serious ones, and know that every word in these pages is written with much thought. No matter where life takes you, whether you're on Earth, Mars, or deep in the metaverse, remember your roots: your parents, grandparents who have faced life with courage, humour, and an unbreakable bond, and your siblings with whom you have spent your growing-up years. And if there's one thing I can promise, it's that no AI, robot, or future tech will ever replace your loved ones.

BEYOND PROGRAMMING – The Unmatched Efficiency Of A Mother's Love & Intuition

Ah, motherhood — one of the few roles in life where you can go from being a Wonder Woman to a sleep-deprived mess in the blink of an eye. Back in my day, we didn't have baby monitors with high-definition night vision and AI-generated lullabies. No, we had actual, real-life monitoring. This meant standing over the crib at 2 a.m., holding our breath, and leaning in so close that if the baby hadn't woken up yet, our sheer presence would do the trick.

We didn't rely on tracking apps to tell us how much sleep the baby got. We simply knew. Today, parents get real-time updates on everything from a baby's heart rate to their oxygen levels. Meanwhile, we had the foolproof 'poke method' — gently prodding the baby to make sure they were still breathing, only to regret it instantly when they started wailing.

Back then, we didn't strap cameras to every corner of the house. We had something far more effective: mothers with eyes sharper than an eagle's. They could be playing in the next room, outside in the garden, or even plotting world domination with their siblings, but somehow, we always knew when mischief was afoot. There was no need for motion sensors — our instincts were sharpened through years of interrupted sleep and stepped-on LEGO pieces.

Feeding time was another grand adventure. We didn't have meticulously curated organic meal plans and dietitian-approved food pyramids. No, we had the classic 'Eat what's on your plate, or else!' approach. If a child refused food, there was no negotiation, only a stern stare that could outmatch any modern-day disciplinary tactic. Today, parents analyse food labels like crime scene investigators, making sure every bite is organic and gluten-free.

We had no smart diapers that sent alerts when it was time for a change. Our noses did the work — like a built-in, highly sensitive sensor that no amount of parenting classes could prepare you for. If the baby smelled suspicious, you braced yourself and hoped for the best. These days, some diapers even analyse hydration levels. Back then, our scientific method was simple: if the diaper sagged down to their knees, it was time.

Parenting wasn't about algorithms, or endless blogs. It was about making mistakes, learning on the go, and relying on instinct. We didn't have YouTube tutorials for emergencies like colic pain, but we had something better — our own mothers, whose wisdom came with 'I told you so.'

So, all you parents or to-be parents, as you sync your AI-powered baby gadgets and debate the latest scientifically optimized sleep training methods, remember this: sometimes, the best parenting tool is simply being there, watching over your child — not through a screen, but with your own exhausted, yet loving eyes.

Now, let's get back to laughing at how life has changed in every possible way!

A MOTHER GIVES… Her All

A mother gives her all — not for accolades or applause, but because love never asks for anything in return. Welcome to my world, if only for a few pages of laughter, tears, and the occasional chaotic moment.

The birth of a child is nothing short of a miracle — a moment when a mother's heart overflows with unconditional love, and the luxury of eight straight hours of sleep suddenly becomes a long-forgotten dream. My firstborn, Shane, burst onto the scene in the whirlwind that is New York City. I was 21, a brand-new mother in a foreign land, armed with instinct, a dash of panic, and a rapidly expanding collection of baby wipes. My husband Astor and I were navigating life in a bustling city far from our roots, and Shane's arrival lit up our little New York apartment with joy and wonder. One glimpse of his cherubic face and I knew two immutable truths: I'd shield him with every ounce of my being, and my quiet meals were officially over. His first cry wasn't just a sound — it was the starting gun for sleepless nights, frantic baby-proofing marathons and baby giggles. Shane's first smile, the warmth of his tiny hand gripping my finger, and the quiet moments singing him to sleep were the simple things that gave us much delight and we realised then that babies don't come with mute buttons and silence is always suspicious when you have children.

A year later, life took us to Mumbai, and that's where we welcomed our second blessing, Thea. The familiarity of home and the support of family made this time feel different but no less magical. Thea was a bright-eyed baby, full of curiosity and spunk. She seemed to sense that she had a big brother to look up to and quickly established herself as the one who would keep him on his toes. When Thea was born, I had more confidence as a mother, but life didn't slow down. Mumbai was a city of chaos and charm, and raising two young children there kept me on the ball.

Thea, even as a baby, had a determined spirit. If Shane was the mischievous one, she was the quiet observer and the mastermind. Her personality shone even before she could walk. She didn't cause trouble; she orchestrated it. If he climbed a chair, she subtly removed its stability. If Shane had a toy, much like a tiny corporate strategist and with the precision of a seasoned negotiator, she would convince him to "willingly" hand it over.

I loved watching their bond form — Shane being the protective big brother, and Thea looking up to him with a mix of awe and mischief.

A decade later came Vanya, the premature, pint-size, fire cracker whose arrival was nothing short of a test of faith. Born at seven months, she was tiny but fierce. **She made up for her small size with a big personality and the lungs of an opera singer.** I still remember the sleepless nights spent watching her breathe, the sterile hum of machines in the neonatal ward at the Nanavati Hospital, the whispered prayers, and my disbelief as I watched her overcome every little obstacle. Vanya taught me that even the smallest among us can wage the fiercest battles, transforming every milestone into a personal triumph celebrated like a championship win.

My children may not remember the lullabies I sang, the fevers I nursed, or the countless times I saved them from climbing things they had no business climbing — but I do. And while they grew into their personalities, I perfected my ability to function on two hours of sleep and the occasional cup of coffee (which was always cold).

Motherhood is a marathon with no finish line, a juggling act where the balls keep multiplying. It is the lifelong subscription you never knew you signed up for, complete with unsolicited renewals and surprise bonus features! Just when you think your duties are winding down, your adult children have a knack for redefining your job description.

The Eternal Worrier – I remember when I fretted over my kids picking up dirt from the carpet and putting it in their mouths. Fast forward a couple of decades, and I now lose sleep over them returning home after 2am. The worries don't disappear; they simply evolve. Your child might be managing a high-stress job, but you're the one stressing over their stress.

The Unpaid Consultant – As my children navigate the complexities of adulthood, I find myself promoted to the role of a 24/7 consultant — minus the pay-check. From career advice to relationship counselling, my expertise is sought after.

The Backup Plan – Despite their independence, my adult children often treat our home as a combination of storage unit and bed-and-breakfast. I suspect it's the allure of free housekeeping, and a stocked fridge that's truly irresistible.

The Tech Support – Gone are the days when I taught them to tie their shoelaces. Now, I'm the go-to person for deciphering the mysteries of modern technology. Whether it's charging the speaker system or a new smartphone, or setting up the projector, my role as tech 'support' is indispensable — despite the fact that I still struggle with the TV remote.

Being a mother isn't just a role; it's a lifelong, unpaid, no-vacation contract. My children became the centre of my universe, and I gave my all — my energy, my dreams, my time, my very self — to ensure they had

the best start in life. And despite the chaos,
the exhaustion, and the suspicious silences,
I wouldn't trade it for anything.

Well, maybe just an extra hour of sleep!

THEN NOW…WHO KNOWS? – From 'Be Home By Dark' to 'Share Your Location'

Every generation believes theirs was the golden era, while staring at the next with bewilderment and a little horror. If our ancestors could see us now, they'd either burst out laughing or start gathering firewood to burn the nearest smartphone. So, let's take a wild ride through the past, present, and whatever absurdities the future holds.

There was a time when conversations were sacred. People spoke face-to-face, argued passionately, and made up over a glass of wine. Today, everything is a digital battlefield. A mild disagreement on social media can spark a war, complete with hashtags, cancel petitions, and someone blocking you on Instagram.
The future? Arguments will be settled telepathically, with AI moderators ensuring nobody's virtual feelings get hurt.

Careers were once simple. Follow in your father's footsteps or find a trade that involved actual physical effort. Nobody cared if you felt 'fulfilled' at work; you just did it, without whining. Now, people want jobs that match their 'passion' and offer 'work-life balance.' The future? Work will be entirely optional, and the highest-paid profession will be 'A Professional Sleep Tester' because sleep feels like a luxury these days.

Romance has evolved in ways our ancestors couldn't have imagined. Finding a spouse once involved a priest's blessings, a respectable dowry, and at least two meddling relatives. Today, love is a complicated algorithm of swipes, emojis, and ghosting. The future? AI-generated partners who always remember anniversaries and never leave the toilet roll empty.

Marriage itself has had a rollercoaster journey. It was once an unbreakable bond sealed with vows, prayers, and the knowledge that you'd be stuck with this person for better or worse. Now, it's an event planned like an Olympic opening ceremony, often with an expiration date. The future? Marriages will come with subscription plans — auto-renew or cancel anytime.

Discipline was once swift and effective. Parents had 'the look' — a silent glare that could halt misbehaviour across a crowded room. Today, discipline involves negotiation, timeouts, and extensive research on parenting blogs. In the future, bad behaviour will result in instant WiFi bans – the modern equivalent of medieval exile.

Food, once a necessity, has turned into a heated debate. Grandmothers cured everything with soup, and no one worried about gluten, dairy, or whether the sheep were grass fed. Today, we analyse every bite like scientists in a lab. The future? Meals will arrive in pill form, and there will still be someone refusing to eat them because they're 'not organic.'

Medicine has been an adventure through the ages. Once, the best cure for anything was a mixture of herbs, prayers, and sheer luck. Today, we have advanced treatments and self-diagnosis through WebMD, which convinces everyone they're dying. The future? Personalized medicine delivered via nano-robots (don't ask about the side effects.)

Entertainment once required effort. People dressed up for the theatre, listened to the radio, or actually read books. Now, we scroll endlessly through streaming platforms, overwhelmed by choice yet watching the same three shows. The future? Movies will beam directly into our brains, yet complaints about storage space will still echo in our living rooms.

The media was once about trusted voices delivering the news, preferably in a deep, serious tone. Then came television and social media, turning news into a circus of conspiracy theories. The future? News will be delivered via holograms that adjust their emotional tone based on your mood because nothing says 'Good morning' like a soothing voice announcing economic collapse.

Daily life has changed beyond recognition. Mornings once started with the rooster crow, home-cooked breakfasts, and handwritten letters. Today, we wake up to blaring alarms, instant coffee, and an inbox full of unread emails. The future? Our AI assistants will manage everything, except our tendency to hit the snooze button.

Politics was once about loud speeches and public meetings. Now, it's a complex mess of online outrage and fact-checking wars. In the future, elections may be run by AI, and campaign slogans will include, 'Vote for me, or your WiFi slows down.'

Travel has gone from gruelling months on horseback to airports with security checks so thorough, they know your DNA sequence. Today, we complain about delayed flights. The future? Teleportation will exist, and people will still find reasons to moan: 'Oops, teleporting gives me nausea.'

So here we stand — at the crossroads of past, present, and an absurdly brilliant future. Every generation predicts doom for the next, but if we can laugh through the chaos, maybe that's the true secret to a life well-lived. And who knows? Perhaps our future itself will become the next best-seller — a wild, unpredictable ride that leaves everyone wanting more.

REBOOTING – Looking Back, Looking Forward

Believe it or not, there was a time before smartphones, before Instagram influencers and WhatsApp, before you could summon a pizza with a tap on your phone. A time when, if we wanted to listen to music, we had to rewind a cassette tape manually (with a pencil). A time before robots took over customer service and still got it wrong. Yes, welcome to the Dark Ages of technology — a time when even taking a selfie is an Olympic event in patience.

Life Before the Digital Boom
Back in the sixties and seventies, there were no smartphones, no laptops, and definitely no marathon-watching anything. Our gadgets were stubborn, required patience, and sometimes, sheer savage force.

The Transistor Radio – The Almighty Box of Noise.
Before Spotify playlists and podcasts, families gathered around the crackling transistor radio. Adjusting the antenna was like steering a ship through stormy seas —

one minute you're swimming in static; and the next, you're tuned into the latest news (or your neighbour's gossip, filled in the blanks if you missed it).

Box Cameras – A Game of Guesswork.
Photography was a skilled sport. You aimed, clicked, and hoped you didn't chop off heads or end up with an overexposed blur. The suspense of waiting days for film development made every picture feel like a lottery ticket—sometimes you got a masterpiece, sometimes you looked like a shadowy ghost on film.

Cooking – A Workout and a Science Experiment.
If you wanted a cake, you didn't just dump ingredients into a mixer. No, a manual handheld egg beater was used, whisking away like a contestant in the "Strongest Arms" competition.

I remember bringing Nans, my maternal grandmother, an electric beater from New York to help her with her Christmas cake dough. At first, she was horrified—how could a machine do what her hands had perfected over the years? But after trying it, she thought it was the greatest invention.

Cooking on a kerosene stove was a gamble—too much pump pressure, and you risked singed eyebrows; too little, and dinner would be ready by sunrise. The stove also had a mind of its own and sometimes decided to go on strike, leaving us staring at half-cooked chapatis.

No Air Conditioners – Just Sweat and Prayers.
Surviving summer meant strategic fan placement, damp towels, and occasionally sticking your face in the fridge for a moment of relief. Sleeping was an Olympic event — flipping the pillow to the 'cool' side and shifting positions to catch whatever breeze existed. If the power went out, we'd sit in the dark, waving a newspaper at our faces.

Entertainment Before Netflix – The Weekly Spectacle.
No television at first, and when it finally arrived, it was black-and-white with exactly two channels. The first TV I got my parents from the US was a monstrous black-and-white SONY set, yet it became the crown

jewel of our home. Every Sunday, the entire extended family, neighbours, and even our maids would gather to watch the weekly Hindi movie. It was a full-fledged event, with people shushing each other and yelling at the villains on-screen. If the antenna acted up, someone would have to climb onto the water tank on the terrace and adjust it — often receiving shouted instructions from below like a control centre.

If you missed your favourite show, too bad—there was no rewind, no recording, just endless regret. And if ever there was a power cut, it evilly ended a thrilling climax in an instant, leaving us staring at a blank screen and cursing our fate.

The Struggle Was Real!
Back in 1983, when we moved from New York to Mumbai, our "fancy" Atari computer was the size of a small refrigerator and had the processing speed of a sleepy snail. It ran on floppy disks that could hold just 1.44 MB of data — basically, less storage than a single blurry selfie on your phone today.

Phones? Landlines.

If someone was using the phone, nobody else in the house could connect to the internet. The horror! And if you missed a call, there was no caller ID—you just had to wonder for the rest of your life who it might have been.

When we needed to make a long-distance call, a 'trunk call' as it was called, we had to wait in line at a public phone booth at the post office, and hope the person at the other end actually picked up. Otherwise, it was back to writing letters — actual, handwritten letters that took weeks to arrive! Until the late nineties, there was no instant messaging, only 'eventual messaging'.

Come 1990 to 2000!
Watching movies was test of dexterity. We rented VHS tapes, and if you wanted to rewatch a scene, you had to physically rewind the tape and pray it didn't get stuck. If it did? Congratulations, you just spent the next half-hour carefully untangling a mess of black ribbon with a butter knife.

And *music?* Oh, music was an adventure! We recorded songs off the radio onto cassette tapes, but the RJ always talked over the best part. CDs came later, but if they got scratched, they skipped like a malfunctioning robot. 'Saturday Date' and 'Radio Ceylon' were the only two western music radio channels with the former aired for an hour every Saturday night and the latter every morning for just one hour.

The 1990s gave birth to the Internet.
Suddenly, communication was faster and more efficient!
The Y2K Era: When Technology Started to Get Its Act Together.
By the early 2000s, we were finally upgrading. Computers became faster. Internet speeds improved... slightly. But downloading one song still took half an hour — if nobody picked up the landline and ruined it halfway.
Instead of floppy disks, we had CDs, then DVDs, and then USB drives. (The first USB drives had 128MB of storage, and we thought that was revolutionary.)

Shane, Thea and Vanya got their first Nokia mobile phones — bulky, ugly, and only good for making calls and playing 'Bounce'. And they were expensive! Every call and text was paid per second and limited to the length of a twitter message. So, we played the missed call game and sent cryptic messages like: "Hlo hw r u? Cm home. Gt food."

Slowly, gadgets became smarter.
TVs got colour, then became flat, and today have turned into smart devices that, "recommend" shows for you. Radios shrank into pocket-sized music players, and have disappeared into invisible streaming services.

Cooking has become effortless with food processors and smart ovens (though the joy of fighting with a kerosene stove remains unmatched). Cameras have been squeezed into phones, and selfies have replaced our careful, thought-out family portraits.

Air conditioners have taken over, ensuring no one ever has to fan themselves dramatically in distress again.

Social media has changed life forever.
As time has moved on, **communication has become instant, shopping has become a one-click event, and somehow, kids today**

need reminders that going outside is still a valid recreational activity.

Facebook (2004): Girls and boys created profiles, added weird selfie angles, and wrote status updates like "Feeling cute, I'm too pretty, might delete later."

Twitter (2006): A place where people posted random thoughts like "I just ate a sandwich." Groundbreaking.

WhatsApp (2009): Suddenly, no one needed SMS anymore. Family groups were born, and nobody was safe from "Good morning" messages and lame jokes from uncles.

Instagram (2010): Young folks mastered the art of selfies, filters, and capturing food from the perfect angle.

Despite all these advancements, one rule remained in our house — the children had to earn their gadgets. No automatic upgrades! Every new phone, iPod, or laptop was a reward for good grades and hard work.

Just like technology, music sound systems went through some wild changes too:

1980s- If we wanted to make a remix of songs, we had to sit by the radio and hit "record" at the perfect moment.
If you messed up? Too bad. You just had to wait for the song to play again.
By the 1990s, the Walkman was the hottest gadget—if you had one, you were 'cool'. As CDs had replaced cassette tapes, suddenly skipping songs became easier!
2000s introduced MP3 Players. By now music was digital. Illegal downloads for music (Shhh! don't tell), and the joy of waiting three hours for one song to load.

Santa gifted my children MP3 players, the Archos and iPods that could hold hundreds of songs! Downloading songs was an extreme sport—it took hours to get a single track on a slow internet connection
.

2005- YouTube changed everything. Suddenly, we didn't need MTV to watch music videos.
2010s – Streaming Took Over. CDs? Gone. Everything was online. Platforms like Spotify and Apple Music let you play any song, anytime. Viral songs became the norm — one random dance on TikTok, and a song could become a global hit overnight.

2020: The Year Everything and Everybody Went Online

Ah, the year of The Great Lockdown. COVID19 STRIKES!
While the world sat at home in pyjamas, technology exploded. Online meetings took over: "You're on mute" was the most used phrase of the year. Online school became a thing; And suddenly, WiFi problems became the best excuse for missing class.

Streaming services replaced cable TV. And of course, the world got addicted to TikTok, where people became famous overnight for dancing badly or making a cup of coffee in unnecessarily complicated ways.

Looking Back, Looking Forward
Thinking back, I sometimes wonder—was life simpler before all this technology? Sure, waiting for a letter was frustrating, rewinding VHS tapes was annoying, and using dial-up internet made us question our life choices.

Yet, there was something magical about it. We didn't have instant messages—we had real time face to face conversations, road trips without GPS, and movie nights where we actually watched the movie instead of scrolling on our phones.

And we didn't take 500 pictures of our food before eating — we just… ate it.

True, we lived through slow internet, floppy disks, and phones that only made calls, yet we were content. Yes, life was an adventure then, and even though we have advanced, the most important things remain the same—the joy of family, the beauty of real conversations, and the warmth of laughter that no gadget can ever replace.

So put your phone down once in a while, look around, and enjoy the world. And if you ever find an old floppy disk lying around… just know that once upon a time, that was cutting-edge technology.

PEOPLE, TECH & STAYING TRUE TO YOURSELF

PLUGGING INTO PEOPLE – Even When AI Thinks It Knows Better.

No matter how advanced life becomes, one thing remains constant — people. Some brighten your day, others drain your energy faster than a bad WiFi signal, and a few make you wonder if evolution just hit pause.

The Cast of Characters You'll Encounter
(Some you'll want to keep; some you'll want to dodge like a bad WiFi zone)

1. *The Real Friends* – The 'Keepers'
These are the ones who'll stick around even when you're at your absolute worst. They will stand by you through thick and thin, laugh with you at your worst jokes, and won't judge you. They won't mysteriously vanish when you need help moving furniture, they've seen you in your 'just-woke-up' state and still choose to be associated with you. They know your weird quirks and still choose to hang out with you, they remind you before the selfie that you have food stuck in your teeth.

Basically, they're your people. Keep them close.

2. *The Fake Friends* – 'WiFi Friends";
Strong signal, no connection.
They're all smiles and likes — until you actually need help. Then they vanish faster than your phone signal in a tunnel. They only text when they need something, they say, "I'll call you back in five minutes!" and you never hear from them again; they magically reappear when there's free food or VIP tickets involved. Treat them like a bad WiFi connection. Disconnect and move on.

3. *The Hypocrites* – 'Do as I say, not as I do' experts.
They preach humility while posting selfies next to rented sports cars. The best advice? Smile, nod, and do the exact opposite.

4. *The Bullies* – People who think they're tough, but are just loud.
Loud and overcompensating, whether online or offline. Block, stand your ground, and let karma do its thing.

5. *The Dream Crushers* – The 'It's impossible' experts.
These are the ones who love telling you that your ideas won't work. *'That's unrealistic.' 'No one's ever done that before.' 'Be more practical.'* Well, someone once told the Wright brothers that humans would never fly. Guess what. Planes exist. So, just give a nod and prove them wrong.

6. *The Kind Strangers* – Surprise angels
Those rare souls who restore your faith in humanity — holding the door, letting you cut the line, or just offering a genuine smile when you need it most.

VIRTUAL INSTANTLY – Smart Stuff That's Sometimes Too Smart.

Very soon, Artificial Intelligence will probably be running half our lives. Your fridge guilt-trips you about your junk food choices, your car refuses to start unless you meditate first, and your personal assistant has better manners than most humans.

Yet, AI is a tool, not a life coach. We cannot trust everything it says and no matter how advanced technology gets, nothing beats actual human experiences — like eating mangoes with your hands or laughing so hard you snort.

THE METAVERSE – A world within a world.

In the near future, we might attend weddings in virtual reality, play cricket with holograms, or travel to Mars without leaving our couch. Wonderful as it sounds, don't forget: you still need fresh air, sunlight, and face-to-face conversations that don't involve emojis. If you wouldn't share a secret with your nosy neighbour, don't post it online and no matter how real virtual high-fives feel, nothing beats the warmth of a genuine hug.

Some Things Should Never Change
Even as technology transforms every facet of our lives, a few truths remain timeless:

- Family Comes First:
  If an AI ever suggests replacing family with efficiency, hit the off switch immediately.
- Prayer Algorithms:
  When life's puzzles get overwhelming, remember that faith isn't found in error messages.
- Believe in Yourself:
  The world may try to box you into trends and data points, but you are an

original masterpiece — impossible to replicate by any algorithm.

So, as we look back on a time when technology was clunky and unpredictable, and gaze forward into a future of floating houses and drone-delivered pizzas, remember this: technology is amazing, but memories are made with people, not screens.

FROM LEGENDS TO LOOPS – A Wild Ride Through Music From The Fifties Onward.

Music has been our faithful companion through heartbreak, road trips, family get togethers, festivals and the invention of TikTok dances. Every decade brought something new; sometimes revolutionary, sometimes ridiculous, and sometimes so emotional it made us cry over relationships we never even had.

So, grab your air guitar, dust off your ancient record collection, and let's take a trip through music history.

The 1950s – Where It All Began

This was the era where every tune was a hit and every twist a chance to show off your fancy footwork. The King of Rock n Roll Elvis Presley didn't just drop hits – he dropped jaws with every hip shake. The moment *Hound Dog* hit the airwaves, teenagers went wild, and parents everywhere fainted in horror. Elvis set the standard: A true musician had to have a pompadour and a deep voice that could make grandmothers swoon!

Top Hits:

- *Jailhouse Rock* (Elvis Presley) – A song that makes prison sound fun.
- *Hound Dog* (Elvis Presley) – It's about a dog or a bad boyfriend. Who knows?
- *Great Balls of Fire* (Jerry Lee Lewis) – Still not sure what this song is about, but its high energy for sure.

The 1960s – The Beatles take over, The Rolling Stones rebel, and Hippies smelled like patchouli.

The '60s was a musical free-for-all. The Beatles had girls fainting just by breathing into a microphone, Bob Dylan sang lyrics that made people feel intelligent (even if they had no idea what he was talking about) and The Rolling Stones made rebellion look stylish.

Top Hits:

- *I Can't Help Falling in Love* (Elvis Presley) – The official romantic song for slow dances.
- *Like a Rolling Stone* (Bob Dylan) – Proof that mumbling can still make a hit song and that being broke, lost and homeless is a great achievement.

- *Twist and Shout* (The Beatles) – The best workout song before treadmills were invented.

The 1970s – Disco Balls & Rock Gods

The '70s music was groovy, as they called it. There were two very different vibes. On the one hand, disco exploded with Donna Summer, ABBA, the Bee Gees and Saturday Night Fever. On the other, rock legends like Dire Straits and Led Zeppelin made sure men in denim jackets still had something to headbang to.

Top Hits:

- *Sultans of Swing* (Dire Straits) – Mark Knopfler proved that guitar solos should last *at least* three business days.
- *Hot Stuff (Donna Summer)* – If this song doesn't get your heart pumping maybe you need a defibrillator.
- *Ring Ring (ABBA)* - **If it was a phone call, it would be the kind where you dial the wrong number and then spend the next 3 minutes awkwardly singing about it.**
- *Stayin' Alive* (Bee Gees) – The official anthem of men who think they can dance.

- *Hotel California* (Eagles) – The song that never ends. You enter the song, but you can *never leave.*
- *I Will Survive (Gloria Gaynor)* – The ultimate disco anthem portraying the resilience d tenacity of a woman

The 1980s – Big Hair, Bigger Guitars, and Overdramatic Love Ballads

The Golden Age of Pop when music videos became more important than the music. Everything was louder – guitars, fashion, and emotions. Guns N' Roses showed up looking like they hadn't showered in weeks and Bon Jovi made sure every karaoke night ended with a dramatic rendition of *Livin' on a Prayer.*

Top Hits:

- *Money for Nothing* (Dire Straits) – The song that made every guy believe that he too deserved a mansion, a guitar and unlimited imaginary chicks.
- *November Rain* (Guns N' Roses) – A song that includes a wedding, a funeral, and the world's longest guitar solo by Slash.

- *Need You Tonight* (INXS) – A hit that makes desperation sound smooth.

The 1990s – Grunge, Boy Bands, and the Beginning of Taylor Swift's Revenge Era

The '90s were *conflicted*. On one side, grunge music convinced teenagers that life was pain (*Smells Like Teen Spirit*—the anthem of people who refuse to wash their hair). On the other, boy bands and pop princesses made sure the world stayed aggressively *spirited*.

Top Hits:

- *Losing My Religion*.(REM) – A song that makes having a nervous breakdown sound poetic.
- *I Want It That Way* (Backstreet Boys) – The most emotionally confusing song turning mixed signals into a hit.
- *Creep (Radiohead)* – A song that celebrates the art of 'standing out'.
- *I Will Always Love You (Whitney Houston)* – When farewells need a Grammy winning send-off.
- *My Heart Will Go On (Celine Dion)* – Even icebergs can't stop this hit from sailing on.

- *Baby One More Time (Britney Spears)* – The hit when errors need an encore.

The 2000s – Auto-Tune, Emo Kids, and the Rise of Lady Gaga Outfits

By the 2000s, music had *lost its mind*. Auto-tune made even the worst singers sound good, Coldplay had fully embraced their role as "the band that makes you cry in the car," and Lady Gaga decided normal outfits were *boring*.

Top Hits:

- Yellow (Cold Play) – The soundtrack that makes every doodle a masterpiece.
- *Poker Face* (Lady Gaga) –The only song that made people *care* about poker.
- Since U Been Gone (Kelly Clarkson) – The ultimate revenge karaoke song.
- *Hips Don't Lie (Shakira)* – But your knees do after attempting Shakira's dance moves.
- *I Gotta Feeling (Black Eyed Peas)* –The ultimate party album that dominated the charts.

- *Umbrella (Rihanna feat Jay-Z)* – Rihanna's forecast for turning rainy days into dance parties.

The 2010s – Streaming, TikTok, and Taylor Swift's World Domination

By the 2010s, nobody *bought* music anymore. It was all about streaming and making sure your song went viral on TikTok. Meanwhile, Taylor Swift had become unstoppable. If you wronged her, congratulations — there was now a chart-topping song about you.

Top Hits:

- *Shake It Off* (Taylor Swift) – The moment we realized she *owned* the music industry.
- *Firework (Katy Perry)* – For when you need motivation, but with extra firework sounds.
- *Uptown Funk* (Bruno Mars) – A song so catchy, scientists still haven't found a cure.
- *Happy (Pharrell)* – The song that made you feel guilty for being in a bad mood.
- *Rolling In The Deep (Adele)* – The song that made the happiest people feel heartbroken for no reason.

- *Gangnam Style (PSY)* -The viral hit that brought K-pop to the global stage.

The 2020s – Nobody Knows What's Happening Anymore

Now, in the 2020s, every song is a TikTok trend waiting to happen, your guilty pleasures might just go viral and AI might drop the next chart topper.

Top Hits:

- *Blinding Lights* (The Weeknd) – The '80s never actually died; they just got better lighting.
- *Anti-Hero* (Taylor Swift) – The song that made everyone go, "Oh no, *I'm* the problem."
- *Flowers* (Miley Cyrus) – The moment we realized we don't *need* men, just a good beat.
- *Calm Down (Rema & Selena Gomez)* – Watch your stress put on its pyjamas and call it a night.
- *Watermelon Sugar (Harry Styles)* – **The summer anthem about the fruit, but with a lot of innuendo.**
- *Levitating (Dua Lipa)* – Who needs the ground when you can dance among the stars!

Where will music go next? Who knows. But no matter what, one thing's for sure — there will always be a dramatic love ballad, a questionable dance trend, and a Coldplay song that makes us emotional for *no reason*.

So, here's to music: the ultimate time machine that takes us from legends to loops, one unforgettable beat at a time.

FILTERS vs REALITY – The Digital Illusion Unplugged

Once upon a time, we had an incredible invention called *Real Life*. If you wanted to share what you were eating, you invited friends over to savour the moment together. Craving a game of cricket or a spirited round of hide-and-seek? You'd simply shout out to your neighbours, and off you went. To see someone? You knocked on their door instead of double-tapping a selfie. And for school projects, you dusted off actual encyclopaedias and books of knowledge instead of endlessly scrolling for "inspiration."

But then came social media—transforming every moment into a 24/7 talent show where everyone pretends to have it all together. It's a place where gym selfies appear flawless even if the only stretch of the day was reaching for the remote, where couples seem madly in love right after squabbling over cold fries, and where inspirational quotes about "God and inner peace" are shared by those who might have just rudely interrupted a taxi driver's day.

How Social Media Tricks You

1. The "Woke Up Like This" Selfie
Online Claim:
"Woke up fresh, feeling amazing, morning workout done!
#NoFilter #GrindDontStop"

Reality Check:

- It took 50 snaps, three filters, and a perfectly angled head tilt to hide last night's party hangover.
- That so-called morning workout? One measly stretch followed by a quick retreat back to bed.
- And that smoothie? Tossed aside for a rebellious chocolate croissant.

No one wakes up looking like they just stepped off a shampoo commercial set. Sometimes, you wake up looking more like a potato — but hey, even potatoes have their charm!

2. The "Perfect Relationship" Post
Online Claim:
"Best boyfriend ever! Love of my life! #CoupleGoals"

(Picture-perfect couple strolling along the beach)

Reality Check:
- An hour-long argument over whether to eat pizza or sushi precedes that blissful snapshot.
- Post-photo, they dine separately—each secretly pining for a comment of "I love you" delivered within seconds.
- The caption might be sweet, but it's just minutes after a heated spat that could rival any soap opera plot twist.

3. The Vacation Blogger
Online Claim:
"On vacation, living my best life! #Paradise"
(Elegant pose with a coconut on Juhu beach)

Reality Check:
- Twenty minutes wrestling with the perfect angle while random tourists photobomb in slow motion.
- Two hours later, lost in search of the nearest restroom and the only word they can muster is a hesitant

"*namaste*"—far from the eloquence their caption suggests.
- They post a picture with a coconut drink on the beach captioned *"Living my best life"*—but they won't show the mosquito bites and freckles on their faces due sunbathing in the hot sun.

4. The Food Blogger
Online Claim:
"Best Pasta Ever! #ItalianFood"

Reality Check:
- Fifty-three photos later, the meal looks more like an art installation than something edible.
- The initial excitement fades as the realization of "too many carbs" sets in, replaced by a watermelon juice for a comeback.
- The restaurant staff and that starving friend? Waiting in vain for a taste of the dish that never was.

Word to the Wise:
Don't compare your everyday life to someone's Instagram highlight reel. Filters may make everything sparkle online, but in reality, those messy mornings, kitchen mishaps, and spontaneous adventures are

what make life truly vibrant. The happiest moments aren't always posted online — because the people living them are too busy enjoying life! So while you sit there scrolling through a feed full of avocado toasts, six-pack abs, and couples who seem to have walked straight out of a fairy tale, bear in mind: social media is basically a Bollywood movie — dramatic, exaggerated, and mostly unrealistic.

No one wakes up with perfect hair, unless they're in a shampoo commercial. No relationship is flawless, unless it's been Photoshopped. And if someone tells you they "love health food," they're either lying or have lost all taste buds (because no normal person chooses protein shakes over Tiramisu).

In the past, when someone wanted attention (like Dennis the Menace) they did something actually interesting — like setting the kitchen on fire while trying to make tea. The easiest way to "go viral" was if we told a juicy family secret, and trust me, it spread faster than WiFi. But today you have filters, face-tuning apps, and an entire digital world telling you that you aren't good enough unless you look a certain way, act a certain way, or own the latest iPhone. Well, I have one word for all this: Nonsense!

WHERE LOGIC LOGS OUT – Social Media Challenges

Once upon a time, challenges were about skill, endurance, or at least *some* level of intelligence — like winning a chess match, climbing Everest or surviving a family reunion without arguing. Then social media came along and said, *"What if we just did the most ridiculous things possible… for views?"*

Now, we've got people attempting dangerous dance moves in traffic, and dunking their heads in freezing water just to prove… absolutely nothing.

Welcome to social media challenges—the only place where voluntarily looking like a fool is considered an achievement.

Some Notable "Achievements":

- *The Ice Bucket Challenge:* Started as a noble cause, but soon turned into a contest of who could get the coldest shock (and maybe a concussion from frozen water).

- *The Kylie Jenner Lip Challenge:* Teens sucked their lips with shot glasses to achieve that perfect pout—only to end up resembling someone who lost a fight with a vacuum cleaner.
- *The Blue Whale Challenge:* A dangerous online game that dared participants to harm themselves. A reminder that some challenges aren't just silly — they're downright perilous.
- *The 24-Hour Challenge:* Hiding in stores, schools, or workplaces overnight to prove endurance, while poor security guards wondered if they'd accidentally hired a team of undercover misfits.

The only challenge that truly deserves the spotlight is the "*Use Common Sense Challenge*" — an endeavour that, sadly, never goes viral. In today's digital circus, social media challenges often feel like real-time Darwin Awards. If aliens are observing us, they're likely rethinking their decision to make contact.

The Unfiltered Truth

So, the next time you find yourself tempted to join the latest viral challenge or compare your real-life potato moments to someone's filtered glam, take a deep breath and laugh it off. Life's best moments aren't captured through a screen—they're lived, unfiltered, and sometimes very messy.

Embrace the reality: real life is far more interesting, unpredictable, and human than any digital illusion. And remember, while social media might demand perfection, you get to enjoy the delightful chaos of being unapologetically you.

WHAT'S IN A LABEL – Outwitting The Brand-Obsessed World

Let's talk about something society loves to dangle in front of us like a shiny bait — *LABELS*. No, not the kind that tell you if your socks match (although that's useful) but about the ones that scream "I'm expensive!" — on handbags, sneakers, watches, and even bottled water (because apparently, some water is more elite than others).

In the past, a brand meant quality. Now, it's about social survival. If today's youth don't have a luxury logo stamped somewhere on their body, they risk spontaneous social combustion. One moment, they're in a group selfie; the next, they're mysteriously missing from the frame. *'The unbranded shall not be tagged.'*

The Great Brand Awakening

I made sure my children understood from an early age that while a good pair of shoes could take you places, it's your values that decide how far you'll go. They weren't deprived (oh no, they lived well) but they were never fooled into thinking happiness came packaged in a designer bag (unless that bag was carrying food, in which case, I approved.)

When they whined, *"But so-and-so has the latest Gucci sunglasses!"*, my response was simple: "*So-and-so is funding a designer's vacation home. Let them!*" Instead of chasing brands, I encouraged them to become their own brand — not by printing their names on T-shirts (which they did attempt once), but by shaping their identity through intelligence, kindness, and talent.

Simple Beginnings, Grand Adventures

We've lived in different corners of the world—Nairobi, Dubai, Seychelles — each move a crash course in survival.

Take Seychelles, for example. Public transport there was a lesson in human compression. The buses were designed to fit 20 people comfortably, but somehow always squeezed in 50. Did we feel embarrassed that we didn't have a chauffeur? No. We laughed, made friends, and got an intensive masterclass in personal space (or the lack thereof).

Despite not always living in the lap of luxury, we had the richest moments—ones that money simply couldn't buy: Barbecues on weekends, canoeing on the lagoon, movie nights, playing cards and discussing our day.

Christmas was homemade sweets, secret letters to Santa (who suspiciously shared my handwriting), and the thrill of actually getting what they wished for.

The best vacations? Road trips, where the car was so packed, we had to inhale in shifts.

The World Will Try to Fool You (Don't Let It)

Brands are society's biggest scam, and yet, people fall for them faster than tourists in a souvenir shop. The nouveau riche and gold diggers, for example, the ones drowning in designer logos, believe that wealth is measured in price tags. They might have a USD 5,000 hand bag, but can they hold a conversation about anything deeper than their latest shopping spree? Highly doubtful.

Meanwhile, the real billionaires?

- *Mark Zuckerberg*: Dresses like a tech intern lost in the office.
- *Elon Musk:* Looks like he picks his outfits in the dark.
- *Bill Gates*: Shops like a dad who just discovered discount coupons.

And the guy who spent his entire salary on Gucci sneakers? He's taking the bus home, wondering why his expensive shoes can't pay his rent.

When Brands Become a Cult

Teenagers today don't lose sleep over bad haircuts or math exams. Their real fears?
"What if my shoes don't have a logo and someone takes a photo of me?"
"What if my outfit isn't a name-brand and my social status crumbles?"
They treat brands like oxygen. If it's not designer, it's social suicide.

The Brand Personalities:

- *Nike Kids*: Always in gym clothes, never actually exercising.

- *Gucci Gang*: Wears sunglasses indoors, pretends to understand fine wine.
- *Adidas Squad:* Still arguing whether it's pronounced *Ad-dee-das* or *Ah-dee-dahs*.
- *Zara Lovers*: Wear all black, drink overpriced coffee, and act like fashion critics.

Meanwhile, the truly successful people don't waste time impressing others with logos. They let their brains do the flexing.

Be Your Own Brand

You don't need a gold-plated watch or a monogrammed bag to prove your worth. Instead:

Stay True to Your Values – Honesty, compassion, and respect never go out of style.

Pursue Excellence – Be so good that people admire YOU, not your shoes.

Be Confident – Walk like you own the place (but pay your mortgage on time).

Dream big. Work hard. Be someone people remember for your impact, not your outfit.

Now, if you'll excuse me, I have more important things to do than worry about labels—like enjoying a cup of coffee that doesn't cost the price of a small island.

WHEN DEGREES MEET DEALS – Book Smart Or Street Smart

Education isn't just about scoring grades that make your parents beam with pride (or your relatives gasp in horror); nor is it just about collecting degrees like cards in Poker. Education is about equipping yourself with tools to survive in a world where WiFi passwords are harder to crack than ancient hieroglyphs and knowing how to calculate tax returns is somehow *not* part of the curriculum. Unlike that expensive designer bag, you *had to have* but never use, education is an investment that actually pays off. It won't go out of style, break down, or mysteriously disappear when you need it most — like your phone charger.

Although education is often seen as the key to success, a degree alone won't stop you from getting scammed at a street vendor. You might have a PhD in Economics, but if you can't negotiate the price of tomatoes, what was it all for? In today's world, true survival requires a balance of book knowledge and street intelligence. After all, learning about the barter system is great, but knowing how to get a shopkeeper to give you free mint leaves with your vegetables is real wisdom!

Schools will spend years making you solve complicated math problems:
"If a train A leaves Mumbai at 60 km/h and train B leaves Delhi at 80 km/h, when will they meet?". Street smart *"Pray that either train actually arrives on time."*

An education can get you a job, but street smarts will get you a raise

In an interview, an MBA graduate will confidently explain their *"five-year career plan"*. Meanwhile, a street-smart candidate will *complement the interviewer's tie* and get hired on the spot.

Schools teach us Newton's Laws of Motion, but they don't teach us how to avoid stepping on a wet floor sign without slipping like a cartoon character.

True, education is what stops people from believing the 'Grand WhatsApp University' of misinformation*:*
> *"Drinking tea every morning will make you immune to all diseases!"*

> *"NASA has confirmed that people with small toes are more intelligent!"*
> *"Mark Zuckerberg will personally deposit USD 10,000 in your bank account if you forward this message to 20 people!"*

But without a combination of education and street smarts, some people would be placing onions under their pillow to *"absorb negative energy."*

History books teach us about ancient wars and revolutions. But they never prepare us for the interrogation at a family wedding:
> *"Are you seeing someone? You're 40 you know"*
> *"When are you getting married?"*
> *"Have you gained weight, or is it just the clothes?"*

At this point, dealing with relatives requires more strategy than winning an actual war.

At Science class you learn: *"Water boils at 100°C."* Street Smart: *"Water also disappears if you forget to pay the water bill."*

Driving schools educate us on traffic rules: signals, road safety and how to follow the law. But anyone who has driven in an Indian city knows that the road is a lawless jungle.

> *The green light means "Go"*
> *The red light means "Still go but honk loudly.*
> *The yellow light means "Speed up or get stuck here forever."*

A person with only book knowledge will wait patiently at a stop sign. A street-smart person will find a shortcut, avoid a traffic jam, and reach home before the other person even moves.

The final test is bargaining at a street market: The highly educated person: *"This shirt costs USD 500? Okay, here's USD 500."*
Street-Smart Person: *"USD 500? I saw this exact same one for USD 150 next door."*
And the 'ultimate' street-smart person: *"I'm a student, I have no money, I just need one shirt to wear to an important event, please help me." (Walks away with the shirt for USD 50.)*

The Perfect Balance

At the end of the day, education and street smarts go hand in hand. A physics lesson will teach you how gravity works, but street smarts will teach you how to hold onto a Mumbai train without falling off.

So yes, education is important. But if you don't have common sense, negotiation skills, and a basic understanding of human behaviour, then you're just a highly educated person paying full price for vegetables while the person who's street-smart gets them for half.

Education increases your self-confidence, self- worth and self- esteem. Education gets you a degree but street smarts are what stop you from framing it and using it as home decor while being unemployed. A well-balanced person should know how to solve an algebraic equation and convince a wedding caterer to throw in extra desert for free.

Besides, life isn't a multiple-choice exam. Sometimes, the right answer isn't (A), (B), or (C). It's bargaining till you get (D) – a better deal!

MIND YOUR MANNERS ...OR ELSE! –
How Not To Be A Public Nuisance.

Manners are like underwear – essential, often unnoticed, but very obvious when missing! Congratulations! We exist in an era where people think "plz" is an acceptable way to message someone, chewing loudly is a personality trait, and half the population believes "Good morning" is an attack.

1. Eating (Without being a public nuisance)
Eating—a simple act that humanity has somehow turned into a test of patience for everyone else at the table.

- *Chewing like a civilized human*: If people can hear you chewing from another room, you're doing it wrong. Close your mouth. Always. This is non-negotiable.
- *Speaking with your mouth full*: It's best to chew, swallow, then speak because it's not 'Bon Appetit" when you're hit with stray crumbs mid-sentence.
- *Soup is not a musical instrument*: If you slurp your soup like you're siphoning fuel from a tank, expect judgment. And possibly exile.

- *Phones at the table?* Absolutely not! The least you can do is pretend to be interested in the food that's served to you. Afterall someone has laboured to prepare it. Save your WhatsApp forwards for later.

2. Greetings (The lost art of not being a caveman).
Back in the day, we shook hands, made eye contact, and exchanged actual words. Now, people think a grunt qualifies as a greeting. Not on my watch.

- *If someone says "Good morning,"* do not respond with "Hmm" That's how you get removed from wills.
- *A handshake* should not feel like holding a wet paper towel. Firm, but not like you're trying to prove your gym membership was worth it.
- *Meeting elders?* "Hello" is free. If you hit them with a "Yo" you better have a backup family ready.

3. Bathroom Etiquette (This needs to be said.)
- Flush. Every time. This is not up for debate.

- Replace the toilet paper roll. If you leave an empty roll, karma will ensure you experience the same fate when you need it most.
- No phone calls in the bathroom. It's just weird. If you're going to multitask, make sure you're at least *not* discussing your laundry schedule while you're in the middle of... handling personal matters
- Time Limits. If you're in there scrolling through your social media apps, remember others have needs too, and no "*just five more minutes*" isn't a valid excuse when someone is pacing outside like a hostage negotiator.

4. Table Manners
- Cutlery exists for a reason. A fork is not a shovel. A knife is not a weapon.
- Do not reach across the table like a dinosaur. Ask. It's a word. Use it.
- Napkins are there for you. Your sleeve or the table cover is not an alternative.

5. The Art of Conversation (Talking without annoying people).

If people start fake-checking their phones or slowly backing away, you need to reassess your strategy.

- Listen more than you speak. If your story is longer than a Netflix series, wrap it up.
- Avoid explosive topics in social settings. Avoid politics at a family dinner.
- Laugh at other people's jokes too. You're not the main character. A simple chuckle won't kill you.

6. Texting & Calling: How Not to Be a Nuisance

- If someone doesn't answer, do not call again immediately. They saw it. They're just ignoring you or must be busy.
- Use full sentences when texting elders. "U coming?" is not how you summon your parent. (and NO I'm not old school)
- No 10-minute voice notes. If your message is longer than a distress call from a sinking ship, text it instead.

7. Dressing (Like you didn't lose a fight with a laundry basket).

- Iron your clothes. Old people are privileged with wrinkles, not your T-shirt.
- Slippers are not formal wear. Dress for the occasion.
- Perfume is nice, but don't gas an entire room. If people can smell you before they see you, reevaluate your life choices.

8. 'Please' and 'Thank You' *(The easiest way to not be awful.)*

- Say "please." Otherwise, you sound like a demanding toddler.
- Say "thank you." Even if you didn't like the gift, pretend. It's called manners.
- Hold the door open. Yes, it's a thing. No, it will not close by itself.

Manners aren't about being showy; they're about ensuring people don't secretly hate you. If you follow these basic rules, you'll be welcome everywhere. If not... expect a lot of "Sorry, we're busy" texts when you try to make plans.

HEAVEN'S HOTLINE – Prayer, A Power Tool

Life is full of uncertainties. One moment, you're peacefully sipping your morning coffee, and the next, you're frantically searching for your phone that's somehow ended up in the fridge. That's when you need prayer.

Prayer isn't just for when you've forgotten to pay your credit card bill, lost your car keys, or need a miracle to pass an exam you never studied for (although that's when people pray the hardest). It's a direct hotline to the universe, a VIP customer service line where God actually listens — unlike those annoying automated ones that ask you to "press 1 for more frustration."

The Many Uses of Prayer

Some people think prayer is only for big things, like world peace or winning the lottery. Prayer is useful for everything.

> • Lost something? Pray. (*"Dear Lord, if you help me find my glasses, I promise I won't put them on my*

head and forget about them again.")
- Stuck in traffic? Pray. (*"Please, God, if you make this signal turn green, I'll never complain about Mondays again."*)
- Cooking disaster? Pray. (*"Heavenly Father, please turn this burnt chicken into 'smoky-flavoured gourmet cuisine' in the eyes of my guests."*)
- Late to a meeting? Pray. (*"Lord, let my boss be later than me."*)

Miraculously, prayer often works — though sometimes, the answer is, *"No, because you should have left the house earlier."*

The Different Types of Prayer

1. The Emergency Prayer – Used when you're in deep trouble. *"God, if you get me out of this, I swear I'll be a better person."* (Spoiler: You'll forget this promise in two days.)
2. The Bargaining Prayer – *"Please, God, let this online order be as good as it looked in the picture."*

3. The Patience Prayer – Mostly used when dealing with relatives. *"Dear Lord, give me the strength not to say what I'm thinking."*
4. The Interview Prayer – *"Heavenly Father, if you could just make the answers appear in my brain, I'll never skip Sunday mass again."*
5. The 'I Give Up' Prayer – When nothing is going your way. *"Jesus, take the wheel. And also the GPS, because I'm completely lost."*
6. The 'Find Me a Match' Prayer- Pray that when love hits you, it doesn't knock all the sense out of you. Pray that your chosen one is not a master manipulator who could sell ice to an Eskimo. And if you ever find yourself asking, *"Is this love or a scam?"* — pray harder. The answer is probably in the fine print of their behaviour.
7. The 'Remember to Call Home' Prayer – Pray that even when you're out conquering the world, you remember to pick up the phone and call home. And not just

when you need emotional support after a bad date.

Praying for Others (Even those who annoy you.)

A wise person once said, *"Love your enemies."* Clearly, this person never had to deal with nosy neighbours, evil relatives, or people who chew loudly. But if you truly want to master the art of prayer, you must pray for others too.
Pray for the ones who talk behind your back (*so that they find better hobbies*).
Pray for the people who cut in line (*so they experience what karma feels like*).
Pray for your boss (*so that he approves your leave request without asking 25 questions*).

And if nothing else, at least pray for patience — because life is full of moments that will test it.

Does Prayer Actually Work?

"Does prayer really work?" Let me put it this way: Even Google needs a strong connection to work properly. Prayer is the same — you don't always get instant answers, but the signal is strong.

Sometimes, God gives you exactly what you prayed for. Other times, He gives you what you *actually* need (which, sadly, is not always the same thing). And occasionally, He just shakes His head and says, *"You can handle this on your own."*

There is one thing you should remember*: Life is unpredictable, but prayer is free.* Use it often.

Pray for good health, good friends, and a good partner. Pray that your jeans still fit after a weekend of eating like you're preparing for hibernation. Pray that you never send a text to the wrong person (especially when gossiping about them).

And most importantly—pray for a good sense of humour.

"I've Been Through It All – And Prayer Got Me Through"
If you ever wonder whether prayer works, let me tell you — I am living proof. Prayer is what carried me through the toughest days, the longest nights, and the most unbelievable situations. It was my WiFi

connection to heaven when everything on Earth was failing me.

So, if ever life throws you into chaos — whether it's a difficult exam, a bad breakup, a job you can't stand, or an unfortunate haircut — turn to prayer. It may not change the situation immediately, but it will change *you*. And trust me, that's often what makes all the difference.

Now, say a little prayer — especially if you're about to do something foolish.

CHIC OR SHOCK – Fashion Fads.

Every decade has its own unique way of making people look ridiculous. In the Seventies, fashion dictated that everyone should look like a disco ball exploded on them – sequins, flared pants, and hair so big it required its own zip code. In the Eighties, people dressed like neon traffic signs with shoulder pads wide enough to land a small aircraft, and in the Nineties, the goal was to look like you just rolled out of bed but in a way that cost a fortune.

Now, we have the 2000s and beyond, where people wear ripped jeans and pants that defy physics by being both too short and too wide at the same time. And then there's the "tiny bag" trend — bags so small they can hold exactly one almond

Jeans: The More Destroyed, The More Expensive

Once upon a time, people would throw away ripped jeans. Now, they buy them pre-destroyed for an extra fee. There are jeans with rips, jeans with frayed edges, jeans that are basically just denim underwear, and then the true masterpieces — jeans that are completely see-through. At this point, designers will soon be selling *invisible jeans* — just the label and price tag.

The High-Heeled Struggle

Women's fashion has always been designed with suffering in mind. Stilettos, for example, are shoes that defy all laws of physics. They make walking feel like an Olympic event, and the only thing high heels guarantee is that at least one woman will sprain her ankle at every wedding.

Men aren't any different. There was a time in the 70s when guys strutted around in platform shoes like they were training for a circus act. And in the 90s, rappers wore sneakers so big they looked like they stole them from a clown's closet.

The 'Barely There' Outfits

Modern fashion makes it clear that fabric is becoming a *rare resource*. Dresses are now just two strategically placed strings and a prayer. Some designer must have looked at a regular top and thought, *"What if we remove 90% of this and call it innovative?"*

Now we have sweaters with one sleeve, pants with one leg, and jackets that cover only one shoulder. At this rate, 2030, fashion shows will just be people walking the runway completely nude, with designers proudly calling it "minimalist couture."

The Power of the Brand

The fashion industry is a magician. It takes ordinary things, slaps a logo on them, and suddenly, they become must-haves. Designer sneakers that look like they've been through a garbage disposal cost a thousand dollars. Or "distressed" sweaters with intentional holes which cost a fortune only to look homeless is peak fashion logic.

Celebrity Worship – The real fashion designers.

If a celebrity wears something outrageous, it instantly becomes a trend. Remember when Kim Kardashian squeezed herself into a dress so tight she had to be *carried* up the stairs? Or when Lady Gaga wore a meat dress? Some poor souls probably tried to copy it before realizing that raw steak in tropical weather is a bad idea.

Men are no better. One moment, they're wearing skin-tight jeans so restrictive that sitting is no longer an option, and the next, they're in oversized hoodies that could double as a camping tent.

The Cycle Never Ends

In the end, fashion is just history repeating itself. The same trends keep coming back with new names. Bell-bottoms? Now "flared jeans. Oversized suits? Now "power dressing." Dungarees? Now "Jump-suits."

Mom-Jeans? Now "High-waisted jeans." Parachute pants? Now "Balloon Pants" Tube tops? Now "Crop tops." Utility pants? Now "Cargo pants." Yes, *these* are back too.

Fashion trends are like bad exes – they always come back, pretending to be something new. So, if you wait long enough your old clothes will come back in style, just with a fancier name and a ridiculous price tag!

WHY GET MARRIED – When You Can Just... Not

Once upon a time, marriage was the grand prize of life. It was the ultimate goal — like finishing school or buying a house. But today? People are looking at marriage the way they look at landline phones — *Was this really necessary?*

These days, couples are choosing to stay together without a wedding, a priest, or a legal contract. Why? Because modern love doesn't need official paperwork, gold jewellery, or a three-day wedding where distant relatives you've never met come just for the buffet.

Let's take a hilarious look at why people today are saying, *"Marriage? Sounds risky. Let's just live together and split the rent and WiFi bill instead."*

1. "Forever" Sounds Nice—Until You Hear Them Chew

Falling in love is magical. You see your partner, hear romantic music in your head, and imagine a perfect future together. Then, one day, you hear them chewing loudly, and suddenly, you start reconsidering everything.

Living together before marriage gives you a *trial period* — like a free sample of a relationship, but with no return policy. You get to find out important things, like:
- Do they snore loud enough to shake the furniture?
- Do they leave hair in the bathroom sink like a bear has been grooming itself?
- Do they use five different spoons and eight plates just to eat a single burger?
- Do they replenish the toilet roll when its empty?
- Do they yawn with their mouths wide open?

In the past, people only *discovered these horrors after marriage*, and by then, it was too late. But today, modern couples are avoiding disaster by simply not legally committing until they are 100% sure they can survive their partner's annoying habits.

2. Weddings Are Just Expensive Family Reunions with a Cake

Once upon a time, weddings were simple — a church service, some food, and a group photo where everyone looked miserable. Today, weddings cost more than a small house get together and come with a to-do list that includes:

- Finding a venue (which costs the same as sending a human to space).
- Feeding 500 guests (even though you only like about 10 of them).
- Pretending to enjoy a dance choreographed by your cousins.

And let's not forget the "money envelopes" situation. In the old days, people gifted useful things — like pressure cookers and bedsheets. Now, they give you ₹1000 in an envelope, which doesn't even cover the cost of one guest's meal.

Modern couples are doing the math and realizing:

- One wedding = 15 international vacations

- One wedding = 100 years of Netflix, Amazon Prime, and Hotstar subscriptions
- One wedding = 2 bedroom condo (which they will have to sell to afford it)

So instead of spending a fortune on a wedding, couples today just stay together, throw a house party, and order biryani — same love, less stress.

3. *"Your Family is Crazy. So is Mine. Let's Not Involve Them."*

Marriage doesn't just unite two people. It unites two completely insane families. And sometimes, that's the biggest reason not to do it.

- Your mom will start demanding grandkids before the wedding decorations are even taken down.
- His dad will keep reminding you about "how things were done in his time".
- Your aunties will whisper things like, "She could have married that

> nice engineer from Canada, but no..."

Modern couples are avoiding all this by simply skipping the marriage part and living in peace. No weddings mean no relatives giving *unwanted opinions, backhanded compliments, and advice that nobody asked for.*

4. *"Divorce is Expensive. Breakups are Free."*

Marriage means filling out forms, signing contracts, and making financial commitments together. Sounds romantic, right? But what if things don't work out? Then comes the great financial disaster known as divorce.

- First, you need lawyers, and lawyers are not cheap.
- Then, you need to divide assets (which usually means fighting over who gets the expensive coffee machine).
- And finally, you need emotional recovery, which includes weeks of

sad playlist therapy and comfort eating.

On the other hand, if an unmarried couple breaks up, the process is much simpler:

Step 1: Change your Netflix password.
Step 2: Take back your hoodie.
Step 3: Leave dramatically.

No lawyers, no stress, just a well-timed WhatsApp status update with a sad song.

5. *"I Love You, But I Also Love My Own Bed."*

Marriage means sharing everything, including a bed, a bathroom, and a blanket that your partner will definitely steal in the middle of the night.

In the modern world, people are realizing that sometimes, personal space is more important than eternal love.

- Sleeping alone means no one steals your blanket.
- Living separately means you have more wardrobe space.

- Not getting married means you can buy expensive shoes without anyone asking: "Do we really need this?"

Love Without the Legal Drama

At the end of the day, modern couples still believe in love — they just don't believe in *all the unnecessary stress that comes with a wedding and a legal contract.*

Why spend a fortune on a wedding, fight over toothpaste brands, and deal with annoying relatives when you can just be together, split the bills, and live happily ever after?

And if things don't work out? No divorce, no financial disaster—just a clean breakup, a new Netflix password, and a dramatic "moving on" selfie.

BEEN THERE, DONE THAT – And Looked Ridiculous Doing It.

Someday, you'll wake up and think, "Nobody understands me. My struggles are unique. My parents are ancient relics. And my grandparents? They probably rode dinosaurs to school."

You will believe that your world is vastly different, that your heartbreaks are the most dramatic, your fashion choices are the boldest, and your mistakes are completely original.

Let me stop you right there.

Been there, done that.

Every awkward phase, every poor decision, every moment of joy, heartbreak, and embarrassment? We've all lived through it before—just with worse hairstyles and no WiFi.

When You Think We Don't Get It… We Do

You think you're the first to stay up all night chatting with friends? Ha! We had landline phones with tangled cords, whispering at 2

AM, praying our parents wouldn't pick up the other line and say, "WHO is calling my house at this hour?!"

You believe only your generation struggles with peer pressure? We, too, had to decide between standing our ground or sneaking into a party that our parents explicitly banned us from. (Spoiler: We went. We got caught. It was a disaster.)

You feel like your heartbreak is the worst anyone has ever experienced? Well, we cried over handwritten love letters, rewound sad songs on cassette tapes because there was no repeat button, and spent hours staring out of our windows like we were in a tragic music video.

You think only your generation stalks people? No. We used actual phone directories to track down a crush's number. If we were feeling especially bold, we'd "accidentally" pass by their favourite café 17 times in one afternoon.

Technology May Have Changed, But Emotions Haven't.
Today there is Snapchat, FaceTime, and AI

dating apps that predict your love life with terrifying accuracy. We had none of that.

But what we had was real:

Waiting weeks for a letter to arrive from a friend or crush, analysing every word like it was the Dead Sea Scrolls.

Hanging out in random places, pretending it was totally coincidental that we were there the same time as someone special.

Dial-up internet, where one mistake could ruin your life. If we were online and someone picked up the landline? Boom. Connection lost. Goodbye, crush. Goodbye, social life.

No matter how advanced the world becomes, the need to belong, to love, and to make monumentally embarrassing mistakes will always be the same.

Every Mistake You're About to Make… We've Already Made It (with less style).

You might think you know it all. Guess what? So did we. And we were just as wrong as you are now.

We, too, thought our parents were out of touch. (They weren't.)

We, too, ignored advice, then later whispered, "I should have listened…"

We, too, made terrible fashion choices. (One word: Shoulder pads.)

If there's one thing life teaches you, it's that mistakes are unavoidable, but wisdom is learning from someone else's disaster before it happens to you.

Trust Me, You'll Look Back and Laugh.

That outrageous hairstyle you thought made you look cool? Been there, done that.

That epic friendship fallout that felt like the end of the world? Been there, done that.

That dramatic door slam at your parents because "They just don't get you!"? Been there, done that… and later apologized profusely.

Life will throw a lot at you—some of it amazing, some of it disastrous. You will fall, fail, cringe, and survive. And years from

now, when your own children roll their eyes
at you, convinced you have no idea what
they're going through, you'll smile and say:

Been there, done that.

And, they won't believe you either.

SLANG WARS – From "Groovy" To "Neon-Coded".

Who knows? In a few years from now language will be so bizarre that subtitles will be required just to understand what is being said.
If I ask "How was your day?" I would expect a reply with something like: "My boss was totally low-gravity cringe, so I had to AI ghost my emails. Major data drain, no cap." At which point, I'll just nod, smile, and pretend I understood every word of it.

A Brief History of "Cool" (or whatever the kids of today will call It)

No — I'm not new to the ever-changing world of slang. Every generation has had its own ridiculous words, and we've survived them all.

The Swinging Sixties: This generation was out there saying things like "groovy", "far out", and "hep." They thought they were the coolest cats in town, with their bell-bottoms and peace signs. If something was exciting, it was "outta sight". If a woman was attractive, she was "a real gas." And if they were upset? "Don't have a cow, man" which meant calm down. (Why cows were involved, I'll never know.)

The Funky Seventies: Then came "jive talk". People weren't just dancing at discos; they were "boogieing". Instead of 'Let's get out of here', you said, "Let's blow this joint." And if something was worthy of approval it was "cool beans", though I've yet to meet a bean that is actually cool.

The Rad Eighties: The eighties turned everything "totally tubular". If someone was a loser, they were "gag me with a spoon". If something was exciting, it was "rad". And of course, the ultimate insult: "Take a chill pill" for relax or calm down.

The Lit Nineties: The nineties were a phat (meaning cool, not overweight) time. If you were upset, you told people "Talk to the hand"- I'm not listening to you. If you were excited, you screamed "Booyah!" – We did it!, "No Sweat" – No problem, and of course, if something was amazing, it was "a bomb" — even though real bombs are most certainly not fun.

The Cringe 2000s: Then came "bling-bling" – flashy, "fo shizzle" – for sure, and "YOLO" – You only live once. My children and their friends were out here saying "OMG", "LOL", and "TTYL", and suddenly, nobody was speaking in full sentences anymore.

The Confusing 2010s-2020s: By the time Gen Z came along, the English language had taken a sharp turn into madness. "It's giving," – gives a certain vibe, "rizz,"- charm as in someone's ability to flirt, "slay," – outstanding / a killer, "no cap," – for real, and "sus"- for suspicious, and "Bounce" – to leave; — none of which made any sense to me. If something was amazing, it wasn't just great; it had to "hit different." If you wanted to compliment someone, you said "you ate" (without mentioning what, exactly, they ate). And if you weren't interested in something? "That's a hard pass."

I tried keeping up. I really did. But when I heard teenagers calling someone "based" – apparently it referred to someone who is true to themselves, I thought they were talking about cooking.

Let's fast-forward to decades from today. Who Knows? A new dictionary will have to be made with words like:

"Neon-coded" – Something incredibly cool, but in a futuristic, cyberpunk way.

"Low-gravity cringe" – Something embarrassing but in a way that makes you feel like floating away.

"AI-brained" – A person who relies too much on technology and can't think for themselves.

"Holo-vibe" – A virtual experience that feels almost real.

"404 vibes" – A person with no personality, like an error message.

"Bio-boosted" – When someone is naturally talented (probably because you'll have genetic enhancements).

"Hologram flex" – Showing off something that only exists digitally, because why own real things anymore?

"Data dump" – An overwhelming amount of information (probably the futuristic version of Too Much Information).

"Quantum slayed" – When someone succeeds in such a way that it defies physics.

If I try using these words, you'll probably laugh at me, just like my children laughed when I said "No Sweat".

Future Conversations (My future confusion). I can already picture the interactions:

Me: "How was school today?"
They: Mr. Kennedy was AI-brained and forgot to upload the test, so we all just holo-chilled."
Me: "...So... it was good?"
They: "Low-key, no cap."
Me: "... I need a drink."

So, although we will try our best to understand, we may not always get it right. And if all else fails, just nod and say, "It's giving!"

WHO KNOWS WHAT PARENTS SAY –
Decoding Parental Language

If you've ever asked your parents a simple question and received an answer that made no sense, you've encountered *Parental Code Language (PCL).* This ancient dialect has been passed down through generations, and left children confused, teenagers guilty and grandparents amused.

The Classic Lines

1. *"We'll see."*
   Translation: No. But we want to delay the disappointment so we don't have to deal with your whining right now.
2. *"I'm not angry, just disappointed."*
   Translation: We are furious. So mad, in fact, that we have upgraded to Moral Dominance Mode, which is far more terrifying.
3. *"Because I said so."*
   Translation: I have run out of logical arguments, but I refuse to lose this debate.
4. *"I'll think about it."*
   Translation: I have already

thought about it, and the answer is still no.

5. *"Do whatever you want."*
Translation: This is a trap. If you do what you want, you will suffer the consequences. Proceed with caution.

6. *"Money doesn't grow on trees."*
Translation: We are not spending money on that ridiculous thing you want

7. *"If all your friends jumped off a cliff, would you?"*
Translation: Your argument is invalid. I win.

8. *"Who's going to clean this up, the Queen of England?"*
Translation: It's you. The answer is you.

9. *"Back in my day…"*
Translation: Prepare for a long, irrelevant story about how hard life was, usually featuring a two-mile walk to school through the floods the monsoons.

10. *"Someday you'll thank me for this."*
Translation: I am currently furious, but in 20 years, you'll be using

these same lines on your own kids.

11. *"I carried you for nine months."*
Translation: You owe me everything.

12. *"You'll understand when you have kids."*
Translation: You are too young and foolish to comprehend my suffering

13. *"You only call me when you need something."*
Translation: Call your mother.

14. *"After everything I've done for you..."*
Translation: You are now responsible for my happiness.

15. *"I hope you have kids just like you."*
Translation: Revenge is coming. "May you one day suffer exactly as I have".

16. "I just need five minutes of peace."
Translation: "If I do not get 30 minutes of alone time, I may run away and start a new life in the mountains."

17. "I just want what's best for you.
Translation: Please listen to me before you ruin your life.

18. "When are you coming home?"
    Translation: I miss you but don't want to sound clingy.
19. *"Why don't you call me?"*
    Translation: I miss hearing your voice instead of just reading your texts.
20. **"*Fine.*"**
    Translation: If said quietly: It is NOT fine. If said loudly: You have already lost this argument. Stop talking. If followed by silence: You are doomed.
21. *Parent sends long, thoughtful message.*
    Translation: Parent experiencing emotional devastation.

Parents will always speak in riddles, and no amount of arguing will change that. There's no doubt that they love their children deep down they love their children but just express it in the most confusing way possible. The best you can do is learn their language, and maybe someday, use these lines with your own children. After all... Who knows what parents say?

SWIPE RIGHT AT YOUR OWN RISK –
Before You Say "I Do".

Ah, love! That magical feeling that makes your heart race, your stomach flutter, and your brain temporarily shut down. While I would love to tell you that choosing the right partner is as simple as picking your favourite flavour of ice cream, the truth is, it's more like choosing a durian — one wrong move, and you're stuck with something that stinks up your whole life.

I've seen people fall for charm over character, for sweet words over solid actions, for a pretty face over a kind heart, for height over principles and for white over brown, black or yellow. And believe me, the wrong choice can bring more drama than an Indian soap opera. So, before you walk into the sunset with someone, here's what you need to know.

What a Good Partner Should Be

A good partner is not just someone who looks great in photos, who towers over you in height or makes your heart skip a beat. They should be someone who:

- *Loves You for Who You Are* – Not because of what you own, what you can do for them, how you look in an Instagram filter or you're the best cook.
- *Respects You* – If they treat you like an unpaid intern instead of an equal, you'll never get promoted to happiness….run!

- *Supports Your Dreams* – whether you want to climb Mount Everest or just binge watch Netflix in peace. If they think your ambitions are just "cute little hobbies, drop them like a hot cake.

- *Stands by You in Difficult Times* – if they vanish when your stocks in the stock market have just fallen but reappear when you win the lottery, throw them out faster than expired milk. Life is not always sunshine and rainbows. If they vanish at the first sign of rain, they're not the one.

- *Can Be Trusted* – because a relationship without trust is like a

WIFI connection with one bar… unreliable and frustrating.

- *Respects Your Family* – if they say they love you but roll their eyes when you mention your parents, or siblings or act like your family is a bunch of aliens, consider it a red flag.

- *Wants to Learn About Your Culture & Traditions* – If they truly love you, they'll make an effort to appreciate your roots (and maybe even survive a family gathering without complaining).

The Red Flags: (Who to stay away from while searching for 'the One')

You will encounter a few… questionable candidates. Here are the types to avoid like last night's leftover sushi.

The Pretender (Mr./Ms. "Limited Offer – Buy Now!")

At first, they seem like the perfect partner. They're everything you ever wanted. They hold doors open, send cute messages, help tidy your house, and agree with everything you say. But soon, you notice they have more personalities than a TV soap opera.

And once you're comfortable, their true colours show—usually a shade of red (as in flags).

- They will say all the right things but never back it up with actions.
  First week: "Of course, I love your bean bag"
  Next week: "Your bean bag needs to move out. Too much clutter."
- They tell you what you want to hear but do the opposite.
- They are sweet in public but turn into an emotional cactus in private.
- They change personalities faster than you change phone wallpapers or have more personalities than a Bollywood villain.

The Fair-Weather Partner (The Great Houdini)

They love you when times are good. This one is here for the fun times, the vacations, and the fancy dinners. But when life gets serious, they pull a disappearing act worthy of a magic show.

They avoid difficult conversations like a cat avoids water.

- They vanish when you need help but reappear when you're being interviewed on TV.
- Only reappear when there's something fun or beneficial for them.

The Gold Digger

They're less interested in you and more interested in your wallet, lifestyle or family inheritance.

If they could, they'd marry your credit card instead of you.

- They ask for expensive gifts but give you Chinese or Factory rejects with brand labels for your birthday.
- They only show love when there's a fancy dinner or a weekend trip involved and most often "forget" their wallet when the bill arrives.

- They try and 'advise' you with your investments but are actually prying into your finances.

The Narcissist ("I, Me & Myself)
They love themselves more than they will ever love you. If they could date a mirror, they would.

In their world, the sun revolves around them (and so should you!)

- They act like they're doing you a favour by being in your life.
- Every conversation is turned into 'The Me Show'.
- They manipulate you into feeling guilty for things you didn't even do. They never apologize – apparently, they are perfect.

The Controlling Partner

This one doesn't love you; they just want to own you.

- Soon, your life starts feeling like a hostage situation.

- Slowly you are isolated from friends and family and decisions are made for you, not with you.
- They get jealous of your friends, your job, your hobbies.
- Tell you what to wear, eat, and do. Their way is the right way.
- Make you feel like you can't function without them.

The Serial Liar ("Truth Is Optional")
A small lie today, a big lie tomorrow. Soon, their entire existence is just one elaborate fiction novel. This one lies for sport.

If you constantly feel like Sherlock Holmes trying to figure out the truth, you're in trouble.

- Their past is a mystery even they can't keep straight. Their stories don't add up—yesterday they were vegetarian, today they love steak.
- Lie about things they don't even need to lie about. They get defensive when you ask simple questions.
- Their stories change faster than fashion trends.

The Victim ("It's Not Me, It's the Universe")

They are forever 'unlucky' and expect you to be their saviour. Always has a tragic backstory.

You're not dating them—you're adopting them.

- Nothing is ever their fault.
- Use guilt to keep you around.
- Has a sob story for every situation.

The Temptation Trap: Beware of Those Who Offer What You Lack

Some people won't love you. They'll love your potential.

- They'll use your dreams as bait to lure you into a relationship where they hold the power.
- They will offer you something irresistible—like financial security, a dream job, or a foreign passport — but the relationship lacks respect or love.
- Make you feel like you owe them for their "generosity."

- Rush into commitment before you can see their real intentions.
- Slowly convince you that you're nothing without them.

Love should never come with conditions. A good partner supports your dreams—they don't use them to trap you.

How to Choose Wisely

- *Take Your Time* – Love isn't a flash sale. Don't rush.
- *Watch Their Actions* – Anyone can say, "I love you." Not everyone proves it.
- *See How They Treat Others* – If they're rude to their siblings, they'll be rude to you someday.
- *Trust Your Gut* – If something feels off, it is off.
- *Introduce Them to Your Family* – Your parents and siblings have been judging people since you were born. Take their advice.

Ask Yourself: Do I Like Who I Am Around This Person? A good partner should make you feel happy and confident, not drained and insecure.

Love isn't about finding someone perfect — it's about finding someone whose flaws you can live with. It's about choosing a partner who makes you feel good about yourself, respects your family and traditions, supports your dreams, makes an effort to understand you, loves you for who you are and not for what you can provide...

Then hold onto them. Because that, is real love.

DATING & DEALING WITH "THE ONE' –
Or The One You Want To Run Away From!

Love is a beautiful thing… until you realize that your partner is a master negotiator who can extract time, money, and sanity from you with the efficiency of a seasoned scam artist. They start off as a dream, but before you know it, you're questioning your life choices while paying for their overpriced smoothie.

1. *The Sly Beneficiary* (Deluxe edition)

This partner is an investment banker—but only when it comes to your investments in them.

They surprise you with "branded" Louis Vuitton shoes, gushing about how they wanted to spoil you and that you need better footwear. You check the label—ah, they're Louis Vuitton shoes, fresh from the night market. Meanwhile, they walk around flaunting their real Louis Vuitton sandals, conveniently purchased with your credit card.

You: "Is this a factory reject?"

Partner: "No! It's vintage."

This partner always, somehow, gets their way — whether it's choosing where to eat, borrowing your car indefinitely (with the excuse that it needs a run), or mysteriously "forgetting" their wallet when the bill arrives.

You: "Should we split the bill?"

Partner: "Of course! You pay now, and I'll get the next one."

The next one never comes.

They borrow money like a government takes loans—never to be repaid. They casually mention how their phone is acting up, and next thing you know, you're in a store buying them the latest model. They say they love spending time with you, but you notice that time usually involves you running errands for them.

2. *The Reverse Psychologist* (Gas lighter edition)

They know you're a catch. But instead of admitting it, they have you convinced that you need them more than they need you.

Signs you're dating one:

They let you believe that finding someone like them is rare, even though they are as common as a coffee shop on every street.

You: "I don't think this is working out."

Them: "That's okay. I understand. You'll probably regret this later, though."

You are now confused if you were the problem all along. You're unsure if you're breaking up or signing up for an emotional thriller.

3. *The 'Your Family Doesn't Like Me' Partner*

This one mysteriously feels unwelcome at every family event, even though your mother made their favourite dish and your dad awkwardly asked about their career with genuine effort.

They don't feel comfortable visiting your home when your family is around but have no problem making themselves comfortable in your apartment, using your WiFi, eating your food, and rearranging your furniture.

You: "My parents have invited you to dinner."

Partner: "I don't know... I just don't feel like they like me."

Although your mother cooked a special four course meal for them, they use this as an excuse to avoid obligations, and soon enough, you're the one making up excuses for them.

4. *The 'Fast-Track to Marriage' Partner*

They believe in love, commitment, and urgency. If you've been dating for two weeks and they've already dropped hints about wedding venues, congratulations! — you've met a 'Fast-Track to Marriage' type.

They use every trick in the book:

Emotional blackmail: "My parents think you're not serious about me."

Sudden vulnerability: "I just don't know if I can trust that you'll marry me unless we set a date."

Mystical prophecy: "I just know you're my soulmate. I've seen signs."

Partner: "My parents don't trust that you'll marry me."

You: "I met them yesterday."

Partner: "Exactly. You should propose soon so they feel reassured. Besides, venues are booked well in advance so we need to book one immediately."

5. *The Insecure Detective*

This partner will never believe that you went to the grocery store without flirting with the cashier. Their favourite hobbies include:

- Analysing the 'last seen' status on your WhatsApp.
- Asking, "Who was that?" after (and sometimes during!) every call.
- Examining every Instagram 'like' with the intensity of a crime scene investigator.

You: "I'm going out with my office colleague tonight."

Partner: "How often do you meet them? Are you meeting alone? Why didn't you invite me?"

6. *The Professional Excuse Maker*

No matter what happens, it's never their fault. They were late because of traffic (even though they left late).
They didn't text back because their phone was "acting weird."

You: "You said you'd call me at 8."

Partner: "Yeah, but mum wanted me to run an errand so I couldn't say No"

7. *The 'My Ex Was Crazy' Partner*

If they keep talking about their 'crazy' exes, chances are they were the problem.

Red flags include:

Every ex is described as "toxic" and "over bearing."

They say, "I'm just really bad at relationships" like it's a personality trait.

They promise they're different now, but you notice their phone keeps lighting up with unread messages from other people.

Partner: "My ex was controlling."

You: "Okay."

Partner (5 minutes later): "Who were you texting just now?"

8. *The "I'll Change for You" Partner*

This partner promises transformation, but their idea of change is updating their profile picture, not their behaviour.

Partner: "I swear, I'll stop flirting with other people."

You: "You said that last week."

Partner: "That was before I realized how much you mean to me."

The Next day:

Partner: Commenting with 'FIRE' emojis on some stranger's Instagram post.

9. *The 'I'm So Busy' Partner.*

This one never has time for you, yet somehow manages to watch entire seasons of Netflix shows and reply to everyone else's texts instantly.

You: "I haven't seen you in two weeks. Are you free this Saturday?"

Partner: "Ugh, I wish! I have SO much work."

You: "Oh, okay…"

(Meanwhile, their Instagram story shows them at a beach party with #Chillin #BestLife)

10. *The '24/7 Job Interview' Partner*

Dating them feels like you're constantly being evaluated for a position you didn't apply for.

Partner: "Where do you see this relationship in five years?"

You: "Um, hopefully happy?"

Partner: "Hmm. And what would you say are your biggest strengths and weaknesses as a partner?"

You: "...Are you about to fire me?"

11. The 'Always Offended' Partner

This one gets upset about everything, even things you didn't do.

You: Laugh at a meme:

Partner: "Oh, so you think that's funny? Wow. I can't believe you."

You: "It's literally a joke..."

Partner: "And now you're invalidating my feelings? Great. Just great."

12. The 'Everything is a Test' Partner

You don't know when you're being tested— you only find out after you've failed:

Partner: "I left my phone unlocked on purpose to see if you'd check it. And you DIDN'T. That means you don't care about me."

You: "...What?"

13. *The 'Social Media Couple Goals' Partner*

They care more about how the relationship looks online than how it actually is.

You: "We need to talk about our communication problems."

Partner: "Wait, first let's take a couple selfie."

14. *The 'I Am the Prize' Partner* (Golden Visa Edition)

This partner isn't just dating you—they're bestowing you the privilege of being with them. They make sure you know they earn more, live in a better country, and basically hold the keys to your dream life:

Partner: (Sipping overpriced artisanal coffee) "You know, I really admire how hard you work despite, you know... you deserve a better salary."

You: "Uh, thanks?"

Partner: "If we were married, you wouldn't have to stress about money. You'd have a better lifestyle, a residency in my country… but I guess not everyone is ready for that level of security."

You: "Did you just turn marriage into a corporate benefits package?"

They subtly remind you:

- They could live anywhere, but you are the one who'd benefit from being with them.
- They make six figures, while you still compare prices at the grocery store.
- They travel business class, while you hope for a free baggage allowance.

And if you ever suggest splitting the bill?

They'll say: "Oh no, I got this. I mean, my currency is worth three times yours anyway."

But when you need financial help?

Partner: "It's important to be independent in a relationship. Contributing towards the expenses gives a feeling of security."

So, if your partner constantly makes you feel like you're lucky to be with them, remind yourself: A relationship isn't an immigration strategy or a sponsorship deal. You deserve love, not an application process.

Love can be wonderful, but if your relationship feels like a survival challenge, maybe it's time to swipe left on the drama. Remember: a partner should add to your happiness, not drain your wallet, energy, self- esteem and patience.

Navigating relationships can be a comedy of errors, but if you find yourself constantly drained, manipulated, or questioning reality — maybe it's time to run, not walk, in the opposite direction. Love shouldn't feel like a part-time job where you pay the bills and manage a fragile ego.

And, if someone really wants to be with you, they won't need mind games, guilt trips, or your entire salary to prove it.

LIFE DIDN'T COME EASY – And Neither Did I.

If there were awards for "Most Unnecessarily Dramatic Life Events," I would have a trophy cabinet full of them.

Life has a way of keeping things *interesting* — and by "interesting", I mean throwing challenges at you like an overenthusiastic cricket bowler. But again, what's life without a few near-death experiences, right?

'Hit me Baby one more time!'

It all started with the arrival of Shane — my first born sweet, innocent baby who had no idea his mother was about to be turned into a medical experiment.

Just weeks after giving birth, I found myself in the Mary Immaculate Hospital New York, enduring 21 days of tests that made me feel like a science project.

Diagnosis? A parathyroid adenoma. Solution? Fly in Dr. Cretchiola a specialist from California. I like to think of myself as exclusive — only the best surgeons for this VIP patient.

Just when I thought I'd had my fair share of hospital gowns, life said, "Wait, there's more!" Two months later, I found myself having emergency surgery for an ectopic pregnancy — on Valentine's Day. Because why celebrate love with chocolates when you can have an organ-threatening medical emergency instead?

Meanwhile, Astor was doing his best impersonation of a working single father, carting four-month-old Shane to his office at 30 Rockefeller Plaza every day. Shane became the youngest "employee" in history — probably the only one who got away with sleeping on the job, drooling on official documents, and demanding milk breaks at board meetings.

Then came my second pregnancy with Thea, who decided to park herself directly on a nerve for the last two months, causing an unbearable, full-body itch. I scratched my way through those weeks like a mosquito magnet in monsoon season. But the moment she was born, the itch disappeared, proving she was already *testing* me before she even opened her eyes.

By the time Vanya was on the way, I should've expected chaos. Sure enough, I developed preeclampsia with my blood pressure shooting up like a stock market crash in reverse, and she had to be delivered at just seven months.

And, because life enjoys repeating itself, the parathyroid adenoma staged yet another encore, this time in Mumbai. Another hospital stay, another chance for me to prove I was made of steel. At this point, I felt like I should have earned a loyalty card for surgeries. Buy three, get one free?

As if surgeries weren't enough, I also took up *stunt work* — unintentionally, of course. While we were posted in Dubai, we visited Mumbai for a holiday, where I lost my balance and tumbled spectacularly down the stairs from the first-floor landing to the mezzanine. The grand finale? I landed at the bottom with my front teeth missing and a haematoma on my forehead — which later gifted me a stylish black eye. Nothing says "vacation" like looking like you just stepped out of a boxing match.

A NIGHT IN THE MARA – Lost In The Jungle

Our lives were the kind that made insurance agents nervous — one adventure after another, often with a generous helping of chaos. From city streets to the wildest corners of the earth, we had a knack for stumbling into situations that would make for great stories (and occasional near-disasters). So, naturally, we found ourselves spending a night in the Mara, surrounded by creatures that saw us less as tourists and more as potential midnight snacks. It was a night of mystery, suspense, and a lot of nervous glancing at rustling bushes; because in the Mara, the only thing louder than the sounds of the wild was the sound of our own panicked whispers.

You've heard of the Masai Mara — the vast, breathtaking grassland of Kenya, home to majestic animals, endless acacia trees, and the occasional unsuspecting tourist who bites off more than they can chew. In 1991, my husband and I, along with our two children Shane and Thea (aged seven and five, and blissfully unaware of what was to come), decided that a safari adventure would be just the thing to spice up our weekend.

Armed with a sturdy four-wheel drive and a questionable sense of direction, we set off from Nairobi. My husband took the wheel while I confidently held the map — although, in hindsight, my navigation skills were more suited for locating misplaced socks than leading a family through the African wilderness.

The journey was long, monotonous, and filled with potholes large enough to swallow a small car. But we pressed on, knowing we had to reach the park before the gates closed at six. Upon arrival, the rangers casually informed us that our lodge was on the *other* side of the Mara. "You'll have to drive through," they said. "But be quick. The gates close at six sharp."

Now, anyone with a lick of common sense might have turned back and taken the longer, safer route. But not us. No, we were fearless adventurers (or fools — it's a fine line). So, into the Mara we drove, marvelling at its wonders: a lioness on the hunt, herds of wildebeest, a rhino that seemed unimpressed by our presence. The elephants trumpeted in the distance, but we took it as a greeting rather than a warning of an approaching storm.

Then, suddenly, the animals disappeared. The sky darkened. Thunder roared. Lightning slashed through the heavens like an angry God scribbling on a blackboard. Within minutes, the dirt road turned into a muddy river, and our trusty four-wheel drive transformed into a stationary object of nature. The axles were submerged, the tires spun uselessly, and we… were stuck.

We tried pushing. We tried pleading. We even tried threatening the car with dire consequences if it didn't cooperate. Nothing worked. And at exactly 6 PM, we realized our fate: we were spending the night in the Mara.

With no mobile phones (it was 1991, after all), no way to signal for help, and a growing suspicion that we had just made the *worst* decision of our lives, we settled in for what promised to be an unforgettable night. We prayed the rosary multiple times, mostly out of fear, and fed the children our

meagre stash of hotdogs and doughnuts —
because, if we were going to be eaten by
lions, we might as well have full stomachs.

The Mara River, not content with just
witnessing our misery, decided to join the
fun by flooding. Our car *floated*.
Yes, *floated*. The animals, thirsty from the
heat, approached us, but thankfully, the
thick mud kept them at bay. We sat in
silence, staring into the inky blackness,
which was punctuated only by giant fireflies
that, in our desperation, we mistook for
flashlights. "Help is coming!" we whispered,
only to realize minutes later that our rescue
team was, in fact, a bunch of glowing bugs.

At some point in the night, my husband and
I — ever the practical parents — discussed
which one of us should be the *bait* in case a
hungry predator came sniffing around. We
even handed our children a few shillings
and a list of emergency phone numbers,
just in case they had to make their way back
to Nairobi *alone*. Not the best bedtime story,
but we were running out of options.

Then, just as dawn broke, the floodwaters
receded, and in the distance, we spotted a

tourist hot-air balloon. We yelled, waved, and considered setting the car on fire for extra effect. Before we could resort to arson, a ranger's jeep miraculously appeared.

They were horrified to hear our tale. "You're lucky," one of them said gravely. "If the animals didn't get you, the Tanzanian bandits surely would have." Oh. Great. As if we hadn't already lost a decade off our lifespans.

They towed us out, took us to the Serena lodge to freshen up, and, after fixing our car, sent us straight back to Nairobi—where we spent the rest of the day *thanking God* and vowing never to attempt something that reckless again. (Spoiler: We probably did.)

And that, is how June 16, 1991, became forever etched in our memories as the night we *almost* became a National Geographic documentary.

LIVED & LET LIVE – Seychelles, The Jewel Of The Indian Ocean.

When we first arrived in Seychelles, it was with a mix of excitement and apprehension. Shane had joined medical college and Thea was doing her clinicals at the Victoria Hospital Mahe. Vanya was enrolled at the International School at Mont Fleuri, and I was mentally preparing myself to survive in a land where lizards ruled the real estate market.

Our initial accommodations — Charlotte Residence and later Michelle Apartments — were comfortable enough, except for one horrifying detail: the place was overrun with lizards. Not just your everyday, harmless wall-climbers — no, we had flying lizards. Flying. As if they had signed some malicious agreement with gravity to ignore its rules entirely. Every night turned into a battle for survival. I wielded brooms, mops, and even flung shoes in desperate attempts to reclaim my living space, but the lizards refused to surrender. It was their territory, and I was merely a guest overstaying my welcome.

Just as I was coming to terms with my nightly horror show, life decided to throw another challenge my way. A month after moving to Seychelles, I lost my father. It was a devastating time, made even harder by the distance. But life, as it does, carried on, and soon after, we found the most magnificent house on the island of Mahé. It was perched at Petit Paris, nestled between a tranquil lagoon and the majestic hills — a seven-bedroom beauty that felt like it had been plucked from a dream.

With our wonderful house cleaners, Gosag and Carlos, we embarked on a full-scale war against the lizards. It took two weeks, many battles, and possibly some psychological scars, but we emerged victorious. At last, we could truly settle in. The house had space, fresh air, and a lush garden that surrounded us like a protective embrace. Life was beautiful.

Weekends were something out of a travel magazine — barbecues by the lagoon, canoeing in the sun, and for Shane and Thea, a ritualistic escape to *Katiolo* for Saturday night clubbing. We had the most amazing neighbour, Irena La Fortune, who took us under her wing and embodied generosity itself. If ever there was an award for 'Best Neighbour in the Universe,' she would have been the undisputed winner.

Yet, for all its paradise-like beauty, life in Seychelles wasn't easy. The rent for our dream house was hefty, and everything — from the simplest grocery items to basic utilities — was eye-wateringly expensive. To make matters worse, there were frequent shortages of food and water. Some days, potatoes, onions, or ginger and garlic would simply vanish from the markets as if abducted by some vegetable-hating overlord. I quickly learned the art of hoarding essentials, transforming our pantry into a survivalist's dream. The only thing that was never in short supply? Alcohol. Thanks to the ever-reliable *Seybrew* factory, the one true constant in an unpredictable world.

Despite the challenges, life was rich with experiences. The children worked hard, I travelled back to Mumbai only every second month, and we embraced the joys that Seychelles had to offer — the pristine beaches, the warm and friendly Creole people, and of course, the delicious cuisine. We made friends with everyone: bus and taxi drivers, shopkeepers, doctors, the head of immigration – Mrs. Telemaque, ministers, and even President Michel, who was ruling at the time. Seychelles had a way of making everyone feel like they belonged.

One of the most memorable adventures I had was teaching drama at the International School. With my friend Caroline, I co-directed 'ial*The Wizard of Oz*,' a mammoth production featuring 333 students. Yes, you read that right — 333 students. It was less of a play and more of an exercise in crowd management. My daughter Vanya played the lead role of Dorothy, a natural fit given her talent and boundless energy. Directing a play with over three hundred children was like conducting an orchestra where half the musicians were determined to play offbeat, some were missing, and a few had wandered off entirely. There were moments of sheer chaos, children who forgot their lines and improvised entire new scenes, and one particularly memorable incident involving a flying monkey who took his role far too literally and nearly toppled off the stage. But in the end, the show was a grand success, and it became one of the highlights of our time in Seychelles.

Through it all, we laughed, adapted, and found joy in the unexpected. Our four years in Seychelles were an adventure — sometimes exhausting, often hilarious, and always unforgettable.

ANCHORS AWEIGH – Ahoy Mateys!

There was a time when cruises were the exclusive playground of the rich and the retired. These were not the party ships of today, where entire families, including excitable toddlers, exhausted parents, and that one uncle who disappears at the first mention of "group activities" set sail in their finest floral prints. No, back in the golden age of cruising, stepping aboard an ocean liner was a privilege reserved for the elite and those who had either amassed great wealth or were done with all their financial responsibilities.

The departure itself was a spectacle. It wasn't like today's chaotic embarkation, where families argue over who packed what and someone is always missing a passport. In those days, leaving port was a highly coordinated, emotionally charged affair. Each passenger clutched one end of a long, brightly coloured ribbon while their loved ones on shore held the other. As the ship inched away from the dock, these ribbons stretched, creating a stunningly dramatic display of separation. The further the ship drifted, the more the ribbons strained until

— snap! they broke, symbolizing not just the physical distance growing between them but also the distinct flair of a bygone era.

One can only imagine the effort required to untangle all those ribbons afterward. Did the harbour staff spend hours collecting them, or did a swarm of seagulls repurpose them into unique nests? Who knows? But one thing is certain: back then, a cruise was not just a holiday. It was a grand event, a statement of luxury, a floating 7-star hotel where the upper decks brimmed with socialites and the lower decks were reserved for those not so attached to the idea of fresh air.

Times have changed. Today, cruises are less about aristocratic farewells and more about all-you-can-eat buffets, water slides, and an ever-present cruise director herding passengers like well-dressed sheep.

So, for now let's bask in the nostalgia of an era when setting sail was an occasion, ribbons were more than just gift-wrapping accessories, and no one had to worry about being seated next to a toddler with a drum set at dinner.

Cruises – an annual family tradition.

For our family, cruises have become an annual tradition — except for the dark, cruise-less era of COVID-19, when we were forced to make do with watching Titanic and pretending our dining table was the captain's deck. But once the world reopened, we were back in our natural habitat: aboard a ship filled with casinos, cocktail bars, Broadway-level theatre shows, and, most importantly, unlimited gourmet cuisine.

The best part about these cruises? It's the only time the five of us are guaranteed to spend quality time together because, once you're stranded on a giant ship in the middle of the ocean, there's nowhere to escape!

By the second day of any cruise, we have successfully befriended all the bartenders, half the crew, and at least a dozen passengers. If there's a bar, we're there. If there's a karaoke night, each of us take turns to sing solos or duets. If there's a game or quiz competition, Shane is arguing with the host about the "accuracy" of the answers. And if there's a midnight buffet, Thea is judging the dessert section like a pro.

Paparazzi at Sea

The photographers on board have a mission: to capture every moment of your existence, whether you want them to or not.

One time, while taking a nap on a deck chair, Astor was rudely awakened by the sound of a shutter clicking. A photographer had somehow found him, mid-snore, with his cap covering half his face. The next day, there it was — displayed in the gallery for purchase, as if he was starring in National Geographic: The Sleeping Passenger Edition.

Another time, we tried to dodge them entirely by taking the less-travelled staircases. Just as we were celebrating our escape, we turned a corner and — click! Another photographer, waiting like a ninja, ready to immortalize our sweaty faces and untidy hair.

The White Party: When It Snows at Sea

Among the many parties on board, one of the most magical is the White Party, where artificial snow falls from the ceiling as people dressed in white dance the evening away. It's all very enchanting — until someone (usually us) starts questioning what exactly the "snow" is made of.

One year, Vanya ran onto the dance floor with her arms outstretched, spinning around dramatically as the "snow" fell. Seconds later, she stopped, frowned, and said, "Wait. This tastes like soap."

Thea immediately tried to Google "What happens if you eat cruise snow?" Yet nothing stopped the people from dancing and having a good time.

The Singles' Meet

It was an unforgettable afternoon, when Shane and Vanya stumbled upon the 'Singles' Meet' — a gathering where solo travellers could mingle, flirt, and, in theory, find true love. My children seemed to have no interest in romance, but they definitely did have an interest in creating absolute chaos.

So, with perfect synchronization, they walked in, sighed dramatically, and announced, "We just broke up."

For the next twenty minutes, they completely hijacked the event, portraying themselves as a couple who had just ended a "deeply emotional" relationship but were now "trying to move on."

"She's an amazing woman," Shane told the group, shaking his head wistfully. "She loves adventure, karaoke, and gaslighting me into thinking I lost my sunglasses when she was wearing them the whole time."

"And Shane," Vanya said, dabbing fake tears, "is the kind of man who always opens doors for you — except when he forgets and lets them slam in your face."

By the time they were done, half the room had teary-eyed sympathy for their "heartbreaking split." Unfortunately, there was not a single eligible bachelor in sight.

So, instead of admitting their mission was a failure, Shane and Vanya did what any loving siblings would do: they returned to the cabin and pranked Thea.

With Oscar-worthy performances, they told her that she had tragically missed out on two extremely handsome, investment banker brothers from BNP Paribas.

"They were so charming," Shane sighed.

"And rich," Vanya added. "One of them even owns a vineyard."

Thea's face twisted in horror. "You're joking."

"No," Shane said gravely. "They were specifically looking for an intelligent, career-driven woman who loves dessert."

"You mean me."

"Exactly."

For a moment, Thea stared at them, debating whether to strangle them or start getting dressed in case she could still track these mystery bankers down.

Finally, she narrowed her eyes. "Show me a picture."

Vanya gasped. "Oh no."

Shane dramatically clutched his chest. "We… forgot to take one."

Thea didn't speak to them for the next three hours.

The Hypnotist's Worst Nightmare

The hypnotist, a man with a deep, mysterious voice and a questionable moustache, strutted onto the stage, promising to "unlock the hidden potential" of the human mind. Shane leaned over and whispered, "So basically, he's about to make people bark like dogs."

Thea, sipping her cocktail, scoffed. "Hypnosis isn't real."

The hypnotist must have heard her scepticism, because the next thing we knew, he was scanning the crowd and pointing directly at Thea.

"You," he said, dramatically. "I sense great energy from you."

Thea blinked. "Me?"

"Yes, you."

We immediately started shoving her towards the stage. "Go on, Thea! Unlock your hidden potential!"

With an eye-roll, she walked up. She sat down in the hypnotist's chair as he waved his hands in front of her face, whispering, "You are feeling very sleepy."

Thea, ever the actress, let out an exaggerated yawn and slumped dramatically. We all exchanged looks. Oh, she was faking it.

The hypnotist, convinced his powers were working, grinned. "When I snap my fingers, you will become a CHICKEN!"

SNAP!

Thea immediately flapped her arms and started clucking like a deranged hen.

The crowd erupted in laughter. The hypnotist beamed, thinking he had unlocked some deep subconscious state.

But we knew better.

"Now," he continued, "you will believe that you are a SUPERSTAR!"

SNAP!

Thea flipped her hair, struck a dramatic pose, and started belting out an imaginary ballad, complete with diva hand motions.

"Wow," Shane whispered. "She's really committing."

The hypnotist, drunk on his own success, turned to the crowd. "Ladies and gentlemen, this is the power of the mind!"

At that moment, Thea opened one eye, glanced at us, and winked.

We lost it.

The hypnotist, still oblivious, took a deep bow. "And when I count to three, she will awaken with no memory of what has happened."

He snapped his fingers. Thea blinked, sat up straight, and looked around, all confused.

"What… what happened?" she asked, her voice pure innocence.

The hypnotist looked triumphant. The audience applauded. Thea played the part perfectly.

It wasn't until later that we told her, "By the way, that performance was caught on the ship's TV cameras. It's playing on repeat all over the cruise."

Thea froze. "WHAT?!"

Somewhere on the ship, a random passenger was watching her cluck like a chicken on their cabin TV.

And that, is why Thea vows she will never participate in another hypnosis show again.

Karaoke

Karaoke on a cruise is like a box of chocolates; you never know what you're going to get. Sometimes, you get actual talent. Other times, you get a performance so baffling that it becomes legendary.

One year, we were blessed with such a performer. He was a middle-aged man with the confidence of Elvis, the dance moves of Michael Jackson, and the vocal ability of a deflating balloon. He announced that he would be singing Ricky Martin's *Livin' La Vida Loca*.

The music started. He grabbed the mic like a rock star. And then—

"SHE BANGS; SHE BANGS!"

It was loud. It was offbeat. It was deeply, deeply out of tune. Somewhere, Ricky Martin felt a disturbance in the force.

The audience sat in stunned silence for a second. Then, slowly but surely, heads started bobbing. Feet started tapping. By the time he hit the third verse (yes, the DJ let it continue), people were cheering.

By the end of the song, he received a standing ovation.

"BRAVO!" Shane shouted.

"ICONIC!" Vanya yelled.

The man, drenched in sweat, took a deep bow.

Was it good? No.

Was it unforgettable? Absolutely.

And that's the magic of cruises—you never know if you'll end up dancing with the captain or watching the spiritual successor to William Hung. But one thing is guaranteed: you'll laugh until your stomach hurts.

And that's worth every dollar spent.

Captain's Night (When I stole the captain)

Captain's Night is supposed to be elegant. An evening where everyone dresses in their finest and tries to impress a man who literally drives a ship for a living. This particular year, I was enjoying my champagne, minding my own business, when suddenly, the captain himself approached me.

"May I have this dance?" he asked, offering his hand.

Now, I didn't ask to become the star of the ballroom, but apparently, my presence had charmed the man in charge of the vessel.

I glanced at my husband, expecting him to rescue me, but instead, he was busy refilling his glass of champagne, completely oblivious to the fact that I was about to waltz with the highest-ranking officer on board.

So, I accepted. He twirled me across the floor with the precision of someone used to navigating a 100,000-ton ship. I was flying. The crowd was watching. My husband… was still at the bar.

Then, soon after I was seated, Astor appeared. His eyes narrowed.

"Oh," he said, his voice dripping with accusation. "So, you danced with the captain?"

I blinked. "He asked me! What was I supposed to do — decline?"

Astor snorted. "You must have made eyes at him."

"I did not make eyes at the captain!"

But he wasn't convinced. "Hmm," he said, arms crossed. "I knew I shouldn't have left you unsupervised."

The next morning, he made sure to tell everyone at breakfast that I had "practically seduced the captain." My children laughed in agreement and said "Yeah, sounds about right."

Why we choose cruising.

Every year our cruises are filled with adventure: whether we're befriending bartenders, soaking in Jacuzzis, getting scammed by photographers, accidentally eating fake snow or tricking Thea into believing she missed out on meeting the 'love of her life'. The real treasure isn't the casinos, the theatre shows, or the endless buffets.

It's the fact that for one glorious week every year, we get to pause real life, escape the chaos of work and responsibilities, and are trapped on a boat with the people we love most. Beyond all the pranks, mishaps, and uncontrollable laughter, there's something special about that time we spend together. And that's why, for as long as we can, we'll keep cruising because, no matter what, it's always an adventure worth every dollar spent.

Ctrl+Alt+Socialize – Surviving Family Gatherings (Without Dying Of Embarrassment!)

Family gatherings are a unique social experiment where time stops, personal boundaries cease to exist, and your entire existence is put under the microscope. It doesn't matter if you've won awards, bought a house, or climbed Mount Everest—your relatives will still see you as the kid who once ate glue in kindergarten.

If you think you can simply smile, eat, and leave without suffering, think again! Welcome to the Embarrassment Olympics, where you are the star athlete, and your family members are the referees, ready to score every misstep.

The Characters You'll Encounter

The Nosy Aunt (The FBI Agent)

The moment you step in, she swoops down like a hawk.

> *"Wow, you're looking healthy. You've put on some weight! Love fast food, don't we?"* she exclaims

> (while pinching your cheeks as if you're still five.)

Next, she fires off her favourite interrogation:

- *"Any special someone in your life?"*
- *"When are you getting married?"*
- *"I know a nice boy/girl for you…"*

Your options are limited. You could:

- Fake a phone call and dramatically walk away.
- Smile sweetly and say, "Actually, I'm waiting for a billionaire to realize I'm the missing piece in their life."
- Pretend to choke on a samosa.

The Relative Who Remembers You as a Baby.

This one is usually an elderly uncle or aunt who, upon seeing you, claps their hands in joy and loudly announces:

> *"I used to change your diapers!"*

This would be fine — if you weren't 28 years old and surrounded by an audience. They will then proceed to describe, in graphic detail, how adorable you were when you had no teeth and drooled on everything.

There is no winning this one. Just smile, nod, and hope they don't start reminiscing about your potty-training days.

The Uncle Who Gives Unsolicited Career Advice

He started a business with just ten rupees in 1955 and has never let anyone forget it. He is convinced that your career choices are all wrong.

> *"Why don't you become a Chartered Accountant? Best profession."*
>
> *"Back in my day, we didn't need computers. We used our brains."*
>
> *"Graphic design? What's that? Can you help your dad with his taxes?"*

You could try explaining your job, but he will only shake his head, sigh, and say, "*Kids these days…*"

It's best to just nod and let him believe you're considering a career in Finance.

The Grandmother Who Thinks You're Starving

Her mission? To feed you until you physically cannot move. You've just finished three helpings of roast chicken, but she looks at you with deep concern.

> *"Eat, eat! You look weak!"* she says, shovelling more food onto your plate.

Your protests are useless. In her eyes, you are perpetually on the brink of starvation, and only an excessive amount of desert can save you.

How to Survive the Absurdity of family reunions:

1. The Art of the Fake Smile

When someone asks, "Why are you still single?", resist the urge to flip the dining table and instead, smile and reply:

> *"Relationships require compromise, and I'm not even willing to share my WiFi."*

Then walk away before they can introduce you to their neighbour's cousin's son.

2. The "Distract and Escape" Technique

A foolproof method: start talking about the potholes on the roads. This will immediately spark a passionate family debate, with everyone forgetting about you entirely. The conversation will soon spiral into discussions about the government, real estate prices, and how things were better in 1985. Use this time to slowly back away and grab dessert.

3. The Bathroom Break Strategy

When things get awkward, simply clutch your phone and say, *"Excuse me, I have a call"*.

Then rush to the bathroom and stay there until the coast is clear. If necessary, pretend to be deeply engrossed in responding to "*urgent work emails*" (even if you're just playing UNO).

4. The Dessert Distraction

If all else fails, stuff your mouth with cake. If your mouth is full, you can't answer any questions. Besides, cake makes everything better.

While family gatherings are unavoidable, embarrassment is optional.

If you can survive Auntie's questions, you can survive anything.

And when in doubt — just eat more cake.

THE LOYALTY TEST FOR FAMILY WEDDINGS – Vows, Wows And Family Rows

Indian weddings have evolved over the years. In the past people attended to celebrate the couple, bless them, and enjoy the food.

Today, many of the guests are there to judge, compare, and start new family cold wars.

Weddings today are more complicated than a government conspiracy. Keep aside love — these events are now about competing for the Best Dressed Guest Award, analysing who gave the most expensive gift, or complaining about the quality of food in the buffet and if the bride and groom are lucky, someone might briefly acknowledge their existence.

Introducing the Wedding Security Booth: The Loyalty Test

To fix this, a security screening system at the wedding entrance would be ideal. Just like airport security—but instead of detecting weapons, it will identify troublemakers disguised as relatives.

Before entering, guests must pass a loyalty test to prove they are attending for the right reasons.

Sample Loyalty Test Questions

1. Have you ever reported the bride's family to the tax department?

>*YES.* Go home, traitor.

>*NO.* Proceed to the next question.

2. Did you tell people the bride could have "done better"?

>*YES.* Your dinner plate will only contain salad.

>*NO.* You may proceed.

3. Did you come for the couple or for the buffet?

>*The couple!* VIP seating for you.

The buffet!. Congratulations, you have been seated at a table where the food arrives last.

4. Did you secretly hope the wedding theme would fail so you could gossip later?

YES. You're under surveillance

NO. Proceed.

5. Do you plan to start a family argument about property during the function?

YES. Security escort, please!

NO. Enjoy the wedding.

Wedding Guest Categories (Post-Test Screening)

After passing the loyalty test, guests are divided into categories and assigned seating accordingly:

VIP Section:

For guests who genuinely love the couple.
> You get priority buffet access & extra desserts.

Regular Section:

For guests who are neutral—neither supportive nor toxic.
> You may eat comfortably, but your seat is near a speaker blasting Bollywood music.

Suspicious Category:

For people who failed one or two test questions.
> Your table is placed right next to the loudest relatives so you can suffer.

Gossip-Mongers and Over-Critical Guests:

Seated at the table with only salty snacks and no water, to keep their wagging tongues in check.
> Every waiter will intentionally skip serving them.

Then vs. Now: How Wedding Attendance Has Changed

Then: People attended to bless the couple.

Now: People attend to see if the decorations are more elaborate and expensive than last week's wedding.

Then: Family members came early to help with arrangements.
Now: Family members come late so they don't have to help with anything.

Then: People danced to have a good time.
Now: People dance only if someone is recording for Instagram.

The True Purpose of Relatives at Weddings

Some people attend weddings only for entertainment.

Aunties whispering, "*This wedding gown must cost so much, but look at the stitching.*"

Uncles standing at the bar, rating the whiskey like it's a professional tasting event.

Cousins taking selfies for two hours, then leaving before dinner.

In the end, weddings should be about love and celebration, not family politics and buffet criticism. But since we can't change people, we might as well laugh about it, or at least serve extra spice in the curry to see who complains first.

SHOPPING CART SHENANIGANS – The Whole Foods Chicago Experience. Shopping carts are the villains of every grocery trip. No matter how carefully you choose one, you always end up with a cart that has a personal vendetta against you. One wheel insists on erratic, making you look like you're dancing with an invisible partner. Another, refuses to turn forcing you to push with the strength of a dozen weight lifters. And as for the cart that glides too smoothly — suddenly, you're chasing it down the aisle like a parent after a runaway toddler. These innocent-looking four-wheeled companions can turn even the calmest person into a frantic mess. Let's take a journey through the real supermarket experience – Whole Foods Chicago.

Act 1: The Wheel of Misfortune

The moment you grab a cart; one of three things happens:

- *The Wobbler*: One-wheel refuses to roll properly, making you look like you're performing an interpretive dance in Aisle 5.
- *The Rebel*: The cart has a mind of its own and pulls violently to the left, forcing you to steer like a Formula 1 driver.

- *The Silent Assassin*: It works fine — until you pick up speed. Then, out of nowhere, SQUEEEEEAK — Congratulations, you now have the loudest cart in the store.

Act 2: *The Supermarket Grand Prix.*

Now, the real battle begins: navigating through the supermarket without causing (or becoming) a disaster.

- *The Aisle Blockers*: Two people stand in the middle of an aisle, catching up on 10 years of family gossip. No amount of coughing, foot shuffling, or "Excuse me" will make them move.
- *The Indecisive Shopper*: They stare at a shelf for 20 minutes debating between two brands of pasta sauce, while you just need to grab something right behind them.
- *The Cart Racer*: Someone speeds through the aisles like they're in a Formula One race, nearly mowing down an innocent old lady choosing apples.

Act 3: The Checkout Olympics

You've made it through the store in one piece—now it's time for the final challenge: checking out.

- *The Slow Unloader*: The person in front of you has two items but unloads them with the precision of an archaeologist excavating ancient ruins.
- *The Surprise Total Shock*: Someone gets to the counter and only now decides to check if they have enough money.
- *The Coupon Hoarder*: They pull out a stack of expired coupons and argue with the cashier for a 5-rupee discount.

Meanwhile, you're stuck behind them, regretting every life choice that led to this moment.

Act 4: The Parking Lot Tragedy
The moment you step outside, your cart suddenly moves too well.
One second, you're pushing it towards your car, the next — it's rolling away at full speed, heading straight for a parked BMW. Cue dramatic slow-motion as you try to stop it before you owe someone a new bumper.

And finally, the last step: returning the cart. Except… the designated cart return area is 100 feet away. Do you walk all the way there like a responsible person? No. You do the classic "*Push it and hope it lands correctly*" technique, and walk away like nothing happened.

And that is why self-driving carts need to be invented immediately.

INTERNET DRAMA

THE GREAT PASSWORD CRISIS – A Melodrama In Five Acts.

Act 1: The Overconfident Setup

You create a password. It's genius. No one will ever guess it. It has uppercase, lowercase, numbers, a symbol, and even a philosophical question embedded in it:

> "T!m3is@N1llusi0n?"

You feel invincible. Until…

Act 2: The First Forgetting

Two weeks later, you need to log in again.

> *"Wait, what was my password?"*

You try:

> "Timeisanillusion" – Wrong.
>
> "TimeIs@Nillusion" – Nope.
>
> "WhyDidIChooseSuchAStupidPassword123?" – Still wrong.

Act 3: The Recovery Ritual

Defeated, you click "Forgot Password?" and answer the security question.

"What was your childhood best friend's pet's name?"

You stare at the screen.

"*Did I put 'Buddy'*'? No, that's too obvious. Maybe '*Budd3h*' to be fancy? Or did I lie and say '*GoldfishNamedPepper*'?"

After 10 failed attempts, you reset the password.

Act 4: The Exasperating Rulebook

- "Password must contain at least one uppercase letter." ✓
- "Password must contain a number." ✓
- "Password must contain a special character." ✓
- "Password cannot contain any previously used passwords."

- "Password cannot contain recognizable words."
- "Password must include a mathematical equation proving quantum theory."

You rage-quit and create something ridiculous:

"Idespisepasswords!!4298"

Act 5: The Infinite Loop

Next time you log in, you forget it again and start over.

Meanwhile, your phone password is "0000", your ATM PIN is "1234", and your Netflix password is still "password" — but, at least those never give you trouble.

And that is why we now just scan our faces and hope for the best.

HOUSEHOLD WIFI WARS – A Tale of Speed, Suffering, And Suspicion

Once upon a time, in a household filled with intelligent yet highly competitive family members, a battle raged daily — an invisible war fought not with swords, but with bandwidth.

Act 1: The Buffering Begins

It always started the same way. Someone (probably Shane) was peacefully streaming a movie when, suddenly — it stalled.

He'd wait. And wait. And then, the dreaded spinning circle of doom appeared.

"WHO is downloading something?!" he'd yell.

From another room, Thea's voice would come floating in: *"I'm just on a Zoom call!"*

(Translation: I have 15 browser tabs open and am streaming YouTube in HD.)

Act 2: The Search for the Bandwidth Bandit

Meanwhile, Vanya would be uploading her music video.

"*This WiFi is SLOW!*" she'd complain.

I, watching from the side, knew exactly what was happening.

I checked the WiFi settings and found a dozen devices connected. One dozen! Phones, laptops, smart TVs, a tablet, a printer (that no one used), and somehow, an old iPad last seen in 2015.

And the worst offender? The neighbours! Somehow, they had cracked the WiFi password (possibly because it was still "password123") and were happily watching Netflix at our expense!

Act 3: The Great Router Holdup.

One day, I had had enough. So I declared war.

Step 1: Change the WiFi password to something un-guessable.

New password: "YouThoughtYouCouldStealMyWiFiThinkAgain"

Step 2: Move the router to a "safe *location*."

Shane found it inside a cupboard.

"But now OUR WiFi is slow!" he protested.

"*Yes*," I said, "but at least the neighbours aren't watching Romcoms in HD while we suffer."

Act 4: The Ultimate Showdown

Thea, determined to reclaim her internet speed, found the router and moved it back. Vanya, convinced the signal was better at a different angle, tilted it slightly. Shane, insisted on restarting it every time it lagged, even if the problem was just bad weather.

And I? I sat back and watched as everyone fought for the last megabyte of speed.

Act 5: The Betrayal

Just when peace seemed restored, a new disaster struck. Astor had to pay the internet bill — but forgot.

At midnight, the WiFi cut out completely.

For the first time, the house was silent. No one was watching anything, downloading anything, or fighting over bandwidth.

It was the calmest night in WiFi War history.

…Until 7 AM, when Shane woke up screaming, "WHO TURNED OFF THE INTERNET?!"

And that is why our WiFi passwords are now longer than Shakespeare's plays and why, to this day, the router remains hidden in a top-secret location.

GPS BETRAYALS – The Lavasa Detour Disaster.

There was a time when people used physical maps and common sense to get places. But in modern times, we rely on GPS — an emotionless voice that pretends to know where it's going. And sometimes, it leads us straight into disaster.

Act 1: Trusting the Machine

One fine day, we set off for Lavasa — a simple, straightforward drive. Estimated time: 4 hours.

Easy, right? WRONG.

Thea, our trusted navigator, held the phone confidently. *"Google Maps says we should take this shortcut."*

That was the first mistake.

Act 2: The Scenic Route to Nowhere

At first, everything seemed fine. The roads were smooth, and we felt smug about avoiding traffic. But soon, things got suspicious.

As soon as we got off the Express way the road started narrowing.

Potholes appeared — big enough to swallow a small car.

The scenery changed from concrete roads to... wilderness.

Shane: "Are we still on the highway?"
Thea: "Umm... GPS says turn left here."
Us: "...Left where? That's not a road; that's a bullock-cart path!"

But GPS insisted, so like fools, we followed.

Act 3: Welcome to the Jungle

One hour later, we were:

- Driving through a village where even cows looked confused to see us.
- Passing suspicious-looking fields that may or may not have been growing illegal substances.
- Getting stared at by locals who probably thought we were lost tourists from another planet.

At one point, we reached a dead-end where an old man sitting under a tree just shook his head at us, as if he had seen this exact mistake a hundred times before.

"Beta, where are you going?" he asked.

"Lavasa," Thea replied.

He laughed. "This is not Lavasa."

No kidding, Sir *ji*.

Act 4: The GPS Conspiracy

Frustrated, we checked the GPS. It still insisted we were just 30 minutes away.

Which was a LIE.

Every time we seemed close, the ETA magically increased. First, 20 minutes. Then 30. Then 40. We were trapped in an infinite loop of Google Maps deception!

Act 5: *The Humble Return*

After four painful hours, we finally found our way back to the actual highway. We reached Lavasa two hours later — hungry, exhausted, and betrayed.

Thea: "At least we saw some interesting places!"
Shane: "Yes, like the middle of nowhere."

From that day on, we learned two things:
    Never trust Google Maps blindly.
    If it suggests a shortcut, just smile,
    'No thanks.'

Sometimes, the best navigation system is common sense. And when GPS says "Take the short cut," what it really means is "Good luck, sucker!"

WHATSAPP FAMILY GROUPS – Where Silence Is Never Golden

There was a time when family communication was simple. If a relative wanted to spread gossip, they either called you directly and pretended they were just "checking in," or, visited your house, drank three cups of tea, snacked on what was served, and then casually mentioned the 'BIG SECRET'. They would wait for a family function, where information could be exchanged like black market goods.

But now, thanks to WhatsApp, relatives can invade your peace at any time of the day, from anywhere in the world, without the inconvenience of changing out of their pyjamas.

The Five Types of People in Every WhatsApp Group

1. *The Good Morning Brigade*

These people wake up at dawn to the ring of the alarm, only to send a "Good Morning" message to 35 groups. Their messages usually contain:

- A sunrise photo with birds flying (usually stolen from Google).
- A motivational quote that makes no sense. Example: Always find time for the things that make you happy"
- An animated bird GIF that refuses to stop flapping its wings.

The real mystery? They do this every single day. Do they set an alarm just for this? Is there a secret WhatsApp training camp where they are taught how to irritate maximum people before sunrise? Who knows!

2. *The Fake News Broadcasters*

These relatives believe everything forwarded to them. The more scientifically incorrect the information, the more they trust it.

> *"NASA has confirmed that standing on one leg for five minutes daily increases brain power."*
> *"Cancer can be cured, by drinking lemon juice daily."*

And the worst part? They refuse to believe doctors or actual experts — but if a message says "*Forwarded as received*," they treat it as sacred truth.

3. The Silent Observers

There are WhatsApp groups with at least five people who read everything but never reply. You know they're there because their blue ticks expose them. You could announce your marriage, childbirth, or world tour, and they wouldn't even send a thumbs-up emoji. But the moment someone posts a factually incorrect message, they magically appear to say:

"Actually, that's not true."

4. The Event Spammers

Their only job is to add you to more groups.

> *"The Wedding Planning Group"*
>
> *"The Line Dance Practice Group"*
>
> *"Final Wedding Planning Group"* (because the first one got too confusing)

> *"Only Family Members Can Join This Wedding Group"* (which includes 500 people)

If you leave, they re-add you instantly. It's like being in a WhatsApp mafia — once you're in, there's no escape.

5. *The Over-Emotional Reactor.*

This one reacts to everything as if it's a Bollywood climax scene.

You post an old family photo: "*Tears in my eyes! Miss those wonderful days!*"

You share a meme: "*In our time, humour was pure. Not this nonsense.*"

Someone posts a recipe: "*Our ancestors ate fresh food, not this chemical-laden junk!*"

They could see a picture of a cup of tea and still type *"So many memories! Missing the good old days!"*

And just when you think no one will notice, you try and leave a group.

Big mistake.

Within 30 seconds, you'll get:

> *10 missed calls from people in the group asking if you had a personal problem.*
>
> *3 private messages saying "Everything okay? We are friends, you can tell us."*
>
> *1 guilt-tripping message: "We may not be important to you, but you are important to us."*

And you'll be forced to rejoin. You're now trapped forever.

Then vs. Now: How Gossip Spreads

Then: You hear family news after months.
Now: You hear family news before it even happens.

Then: One person tells the gossip, and it spreads slowly.
Now: One WhatsApp message, and 50 people know instantly.
Then: Someone used to visit for tea to share news. Now: Someone sends a

message, then five minutes later asks, 'No reply?'

It's true that WhatsApp helps connect people, and makes life easier. But it has also given people unlimited power.

The only way to survive? Mute notifications and pretend you didn't see anything although they'll know anyway!

MIRROR MIRROR ON THE WALL –
Nothing Lasts Forever

Once upon a time (not that long ago), I had the energy of a child at a birthday party who just spotted the cake. I could climb trees, hop over puddles, and sit cross-legged for hours without my legs going numb. My face was smooth, my hair had a mind of its own but at least stayed on my head, and my knees didn't sound like a rusty door hinge every time I bent them.

Now? Let's just say things have evolved.

The Curious Case of the Vanishing Smile

When I flip through old photographs, I see a younger me smiling effortlessly, looking fresh and carefree. These days, when posing for a picture, my daughter Thea has to remind me to smile with my lips in an upward direction — as if I'm a malfunctioning robot who needs a manual reset. Apparently, somewhere along the way, my face forgot that smiles go up, not straight ahead like a passport photo. And anytime I try and take a selfie — by the time I find a flattering angle, my arms ache, my phone is in danger of falling on my face, and I've given up on the whole idea.

The Fine Lines of Motherhood

Then, there's the mirror. I look at my forehead and see fine lines — each one telling a story of a sleepless night spent worrying about my children.

They insist I shouldn't worry now that they're 'adults', as if motherhood comes with an expiration date. "*Mum, you don't have to worry about us anymore.*" Oh, sure. That's like telling a fish not to swim or me not to double-check if the gas is off before leaving the house. Worrying is practically my hobby at this point.

If one child is traveling, I imagine every possible scenario, from lost luggage to them accidentally missing the flight. If another child says, "*I'll tell you later*", my brain immediately drafts a 300-page suspense thriller about what it could be. And if any of them make a decision, well, let's just say I need a drink, a deep breath, and sometimes, divine intervention.

Being a mother means worrying — whether they're crossing the road or crossing into questionable life decisions.

My Knees Have Resigned

Once upon a time, my knees were my best friends. They supported every adventure,

Every squat and every tree climb.

Now, they have resigned from their duties without so much as a farewell speech.

I used to climb stools without thinking. Now, climbing a stool is a strategic mission.

> *Step one:* Find something sturdy to hold onto.
> *Step two*: Assess the risk of falling versus the importance of the item I'm reaching for.
> *Step three*: Have an emergency plan in case things go wrong.
> *Step four*: Wonder why I even stored things this high in the first place.

And should my children find me standing on a stool, all hell breaks lose.

Sitting on the floor? A disaster waiting to happen. I used to pop up like a jack-in-the-box. Now, getting up requires advanced planning, proper breathing techniques, and sometimes, an extra hand for support. If I sit cross-legged for too long, my legs fall so deeply asleep that I practically need to send them a wake-up call.

And kneeling in church? Oh, that used to be a peaceful moment of prayer. Now, when I get up, it's a public event. My knees crack loud enough to echo through the pews, and I grip the bench like I'm recovering from an intense gym session complete with sound effects.

The Unpredictable Body

It's not just my knees that have developed a rebellious streak. My back also enjoys surprising me. Sometimes, I bend down to pick up something, and my back whispers, *"Oh? You think you're coming back up that easily"? Interesting."* I sleep in the wrong position, and I wake up feeling like I've been thrown off a moving train.

Even eating has become unpredictable. Once upon a time, I could eat anything at any hour. Now, I eat out of time, and my stomach holds a protest rally all night. Spicy food? Love it. Does it love me back? No. It haunts me.

The Battle of Comfort vs. Style

There was a time when I would wear fancy shoes no matter what. High 4-inch stiletto heels? No problem. Tight jeans? Bring it on. Now, I prioritize comfort over fashion. Shoes must be soft, cushioned, and slip-on wedges. Clothes? If it requires too much effort to put on, I don't want it. And carrying a handbag — if it's too heavy, I start evaluating what I really need in life.

What Lasts Forever?
While my knees may protest, my smile may need occasional reminders, and my back may issue random warnings, my inner being is still the same.

True, nothing lasts forever — not my tree-climbing days, not my ability to jump off a stool without consequences, and not my ability to eat at any time of the day or night without regrets. But the love of family and contentment lasts forever. And as long as I can still laugh at myself, I'd say I'm doing just fine.

OOPS! MY BAD... Love, Mum

Back in the day, parenting was a no-nonsense business. There were no books on "gentle parenting" or "positive reinforcement." Discipline was swift, effective, and sometimes airborne (like the flying slipper).

The Death Stare: No words needed. One look from a parent could make a child forget their own name.

The Weapon of Choice: Slippers, wooden spoons, belts, canes, hangers — everyday household items doubled as behaviour-correcting devices.

The Fear of "Wait till Your Father Comes Home": Even if Dad was the 'chill' one, the idea of him knowing was enough to straighten up a child.

Public Shame: Parents in those days had no problem disciplining kids in front of the entire grocery store. They could smack you in aisle 5 and then ask, "*What brand of biscuits do you want?*" like nothing happened.

And the best part? If you dared to complain to another adult, they'd just say, "Good! You probably deserved it!"

Today: The Negotiation Era

Parenting today is like a hostage negotiation. Instead of discipline, there are "conversations."

"*Let's use our words*": Instead of "Stop that right now!" it's "Sweetie, let's talk about why hitting your sister isn't a good choice."

Time-Outs Instead of Smacks: Instead of the instant justice of a slap, modern parents say, "*Go sit in the corner and think about what you did.*" A chance for the kids to plot their next move.

Apologizing to Kids: If today's parents accidentally raise their voice, they feel guilty and hold a family meeting to discuss everyone's feelings.

Kids Have More Rights Than Employees: If you yell at your child, they ask you to "*Calm down*", remind you of "*gentle parenting*" and might even Google child protection laws just to scare you.

I followed the tried and tested methods of my time.

The Flying Hand: My hand had a mind of its own. It could smack the back of a child's head before they even realized they were in trouble. (Reflexes like a ninja.)

The Threats That Worked: "I'll send you to boarding school!" (No intention of doing so, but fear is a great teacher.)

Comparisons: "Look at 'so and so's' son — he's so obedient!" (Classic.)

Grounding: When I grounded them, they actually suffered. No PlayStation, no going out — just a book and their own miserable thoughts.

Cursing in Frustration: Oh yes, I cursed. Sometimes under my breath, sometimes very loudly. And my kids learned new vocabulary faster than learning Hindi and French.

Yet my love for them never changed.

Yes, I smacked, I cursed, I compared — but I also loved them fiercely. I cooked for them, fought for them, celebrated their wins, and prayed for them. And despite all the threats I made, none of them actually ended up in boarding school.

Now, when they tell stories about their childhood, they laugh. And if they can laugh about it, then maybe — just maybe — I did okay.

WASN'T IT JUST YESTERDAY – Old School Mum

Time moves faster than we can ever imagine. One moment, you are the child, holding your parent's hand; the next, you are the adult, guiding your own. But no matter how much time passes, you will always be someone's child, someone's cherished little one.

Wasn't it just yesterday, that I held their tiny fingers, teaching them to wrap them around mine? Wasn't it just yesterday, that I spent hours bending over a walker, coaxing them to take their first wobbly steps, only to have them fall on their diaper-cushioned behinds and laugh like they had discovered a new game? Wasn't it just yesterday, that I sat cross-legged on the floor, clapping and cheering every time they managed to say something resembling a word — like "mama" or "dada" — even though, in hindsight, they were probably just trying to clear their throat?

I remember the sleepless nights, rocking them in my arms, singing lullabies in various keys, hoping they would sleep before I did.

The toddler years were a blur of spills, tears, and endless rounds of "Why?"

"Why is the sky blue?"
"Because of light scattering."
"Why does light scatter?"
"Because it's made of tiny particles."
"Why is it made of tiny particles?"
"Because... because... OH LOOK, A BIRD!"

I cooked meals that catered to their ever-changing moods—cutting sandwiches into stars and sometimes, abstract modern art when the knife slipped. I packed lunch boxes with their favourite treats hoping they would eat something other than another child's food.

Homework? Oh, that was a battlefield. Teaching math meant rediscovering my long-lost childhood trauma of fractions. Teaching English meant trying to explain why "knife" has a "k" that refuses to be pronounced. And science—let's not get into that-I actually bought a gold fish to explain its anatomy (and later had to get permissions from airport security to carry the fish from Dubai to Mumbai)

And then came the teenage years. Doors slammed. Eyes rolled. My IQ apparently dropped by 50 points overnight.

> *"Mum, you don't get it."*
> *"Mum, this is how things are done now."*
> *"Mum, please, stop talking like it's the 1800s."*

Excuse me? The 1800s? I wasn't sending them to milk cows and churn butter. I was just suggesting they wake up before noon! And now, the tables have turned. It's a full circle. The same children who once needed me to cut their food into bite-sized pieces now lecture me on my diet.

> *"Mom, avoid sugar."*
> "But I just—"
> *"Mom, eat cauliflower rice."*
> "What's wrong with normal basmati rice?"
> *"Mom, did you exercise today?"*
> "I climbed the stairs."
> *"That's not exercise."*
> "Then what was it? Teleportation?"

They have fitness routines planned,

and strict rules about what I should and shouldn't do. Meanwhile, they spend hours on their phones, their fingers moving at lightning speed, their eyes glued to the screen. Yet, calling home every day is not a necessity.
"Mom, I was busy."
"Too busy to say hello?"
"I was on work calls."
"And after work calls?"
"I was on call with a friend."
"But you text them all day!"
"That's different."

Oh yes, it's different. Everything is different now. They make their own decisions because, apparently, I'm "*old school.*" I don't understand the new trends, the way things work, the new lingo, or why avocado toast costs more a bottle of champagne.
But deep down, I know they still need me. Because when a favourite recipe needs to be made just right, or when life throws them a problem too big to solve on their own, or they need prayers or even a bit of *'luck'* guess who they call?

That's right. *Old-school Mom!*

THE UNTOLD TALES –

And it's a wrap! Or is it? There are still untold tales in the archives of my mind that might make you question reality itself. If your curiosity is itching, find me on Instagram at lyncia_official Who knows? I might just spill the beans, accidentally of course!

www.ingramcontent.com/pod-product-compliance
Lightning Source LLC
LaVergne TN
LVHW061611070526
838199LV00078B/7244